GENDER PIONEERS

of related interest

Transitions
Our Stories of Being Trans
Various Authors
Forewords by Meg-John Barker, Juno Roche and Sabah Choudrey
ISBN 978 1 78775 851 3
eISBN 978 1 78775 852 0

Non-Binary Lives
An Anthology of Intersecting Identities
Edited by Jos Twist, Ben Vincent, Meg-John Barker and Kat Gupta
ISBN 978 1 78775 339 6
eISBN 978 1 78775 340 2

Coming Out Stories
Edited by Emma Goswell and Sam Walker
Foreword by Tim Sigsworth MBE
ISBN 978 1 78775 495 9
eISBN 978 1 78775 496 6

The A–Z of Gender and Sexuality
From Ace to Ze
Morgan Lev Edward Holleb
ISBN 978 1 78592 342 5
eISBN 978 1 78450 663 6

GENDER PIONEERS

A Celebration of Transgender, Non-Binary and Intersex Icons

Philippa Punchard

Illustrated by Philippa Punchard
Foreword by Christine Burns MBE

Jessica Kingsley Publishers
London and Philadelphia

First published in Great Britain in 2022 by Jessica Kingsley Publishers
An imprint of Hodder & Stoughton Ltd
An Hachette Company

1

A CIP catalogue record for this title is available from the
British Library and the Library of Congress

ISBN 978 1 78775 515 4
eISBN 978 1 78775514 7

Printed and bound in China by Leo Paper Products Ltd

Jessica Kingsley Publishers' policy is to use papers that are natural,
renewable and recyclable products and made from wood grown
in sustainable forests. The logging and manufacturing processes
are expected to conform to the environmental regulations
of the country of origin.

Jessica Kingsley Publishers
Carmelite House
50 Victoria Embankment
London EC4Y 0DZ

www.jkp.com

For Vini, Lois and Kaspa

Foreword

There is a mantra that trans people often find themselves repeating, particularly during the Western world's backlash to our existence that has been pushed to the fore over the last four to five years: Trans people are not a new thing. Let's put that in capitals:

TRANS PEOPLE ARE NOT A NEW THING

You may think otherwise, but that says more about you than about us.

Trans people are not a product or symptom of some kind of Western liberal decadence – though we Western liberals probably spend a disproportionate amount of time worrying over a political decay that sees humanity losing a grip on the truth and ignoring science and the lessons of history (or even what a famous politician said last week) just as we are faced with arguably the greatest existential challenges in 80 years. No. Trans people are not a Western thing – you'll find us with different names and places in societies right around the world.

Once more for those at the back: We are not new. We are not a fad. We've been here as long as humans have had a word for 'here'.

Of course, the result of that defiant proclamation is that sceptics will always roll up to demand proof. Fair enough; you shouldn't just take anyone's word, even if they're spinning an attractive-sounding conspiracy theory about billionaires and pharmaceutical profits. This is why I refer to the 'always here, everywhere' proclamation as a mantra, because we have to keep repeating it and presenting the receipts. For some reason, Western society, even when they're old enough to know better, has a habit of forgetting, or demanding more examples, or claiming our examples mean something else and aren't proof of our universality at all.

When I was born in 1954, British papers were titillated by the stories reported of a former World War II fighter pilot who had 'changed sex' and was now called Roberta Cowell (1918–2011). It certainly wasn't the first such story. The whole world had not long since processed the news of an American former GI, who came back from treatment in Denmark as Christine Jorgensen (1926–1989). Both of these pioneering trans women are featured in this book. Yet when today's sceptics argue in all seriousness that being trans is a modern fad (caused by social media or something), these examples – as old as I am – are conveniently forgotten or discounted, along with other examples such as Dr Laurence Michael Dillon (1915–1962, also featured in this book) or contemporaries such as April Ashley (still alive to tell the tale), Jacqueline Dufresnoy aka Coccinelle (1931–2006) and Jan Morris (1926–2020).

I mention these names in particular not because they're the only examples of their time – far from it – but because the history of minorities tends to be incomplete and to rely on those figures that are initially famous in the press or justice system. These are the ones that I gradually learned about in my childhood and adolescence, from the newspapers or from the first other real-life trans people I managed to meet. I learned about April Ashley from a Sunday tabloid when I was twelve. For eight years she was my only reference point. In 1974, I (aged twenty) learned about Jan Morris – the first trans person to have the agency to write an autobiography. Shortly after that, I met a precious few other trans people and learned, from them, the name of the Chevalier d'Éon (1728–1810), whose antiquity raised the tantalizing question of just how long had we been around? What lay between this one curious apparent outlier from the late 18th century and the living examples that said I wasn't alone?

In evidential terms, this long gap was admittedly a problem. Was the controversial sword fighting diplomat and spy a trans person in the way I knew? We didn't have that word in those days. Medicine gave us the terms transvestite, for someone who periodically cross-dresses, and transsexual, the people who were like those famous cases of Jorgensen, Cowell, Dillon, Ashley, Morris (and little information-starved me and my friends). The only thing I knew about intersex people was from a tiny section in the school biology textbook when I was thirteen. Nobody had coined the words non-binary or transgender. We didn't have the internet or web in those days. I wasn't an historian (not then, at any rate). How could I or any trans person in those days advance the idea that we might be anything other than a recent product of post-war doctors getting carried away? That's what the sceptics would say. Genuinely, in the 1960s, '70s and even the '80s, we had nothing with which to push back on the dismissive assertion that we were a late 20th century anomaly – a medical fad that ought to be closed down rather than 'humoured' or even respected.

In hindsight, with the experience of helping to excavate the untold histories of other minorities, I can see many parallels. In 2009, I came across the first attempt I had seen by anyone to catalogue a list of historical gay, lesbian and bisexual figures (plus the most obvious and inescapable trans names). It was produced by the PCS Union for LGBT History Month that year. The consensus seemed to be that this was pretty groundbreaking. In 2011, inspired by this, I helped get the NHS to commission what is now the LGBT Foundation, and a small trans group, to build on that first attempt by conducting actual research. The researchers soon uncovered far more – enough to fill a 35-page booklet. A couple of years later, we repeated this exercise for disabled people, realizing that they too had very little history to go on – certainly not history seen through the eyes of disabled people instead of self-congratulating and pathologizing philanthropists. That exercise, led by disabled people themselves, produced an even thicker booklet of almost 50 pages – a revelation to almost everyone (not that we doubted in this case that there had always been disabled people). With minority histories, as in archaeology, the more you dig, the more you find.

Despite efforts like these, finding specifics about the lives of minorities of any kind felt like hard work. This was knowledge that the white, male-dominated, straight, able-bodied, cisgender world had never thought worth writing down, except as seen through their own lens. The Chevalier d'Éon was remembered, for instance, because of the public interest in determining what they thought to be her 'true' sex when they died. This was deemed important as there were bets riding on the results. If any other trans, non-binary or intersex people were around in that era, or since, would anyone have written down details that survived to be researched? What form would those accounts take? We've already encountered the role of the press. It turns out the judiciary had a very specific interest, too, as we'll see shortly.

So far I've mentioned names mostly from the last 70 years. But what about earlier than that? What about the first half of the 20th century?

Well, it turns out that there are plenty of examples, many whom have passed away now and so qualify for mentions in this book. One name that has latterly attracted more attention is that of Lily Elbe (1882–1931), because her story received the Hollywood treatment in a film starring Eddie Redmayne. People are less likely to have heard of her contemporary Dora Richter (1891–1933) – believed to be the first to undergo surgical and hormonal male to female (MTF) gender reassignment. Dora and Lily were both patients of Dr Magnus Hirschfeld, the German physician and sexologist who first pioneered the study of what he dubbed in 1923 'transexuallismus', as opposed to sexual orientation, with which it had formerly been lumped. Dr Hirschfeld's work led to those first surgeries but was detested by the emerging Nazi machine. As a Jew, he himself was forced to flee Germany and his Institute für Sexualwissenschaft was sacked and the records destroyed in book burning rallies in 1933. Dora and others were killed. We can only speculate how differently trans history may have turned out had it not been for this destruction of lives and research, followed by a world war.

Despite this setback, there are a surprising number of examples of gender crossing to be found in the 1930s and 1940s. One example you can read here is that of Colonel Victor Barker (1895–1960), a colourful character whom you can research from both newspaper and judicial records. His 1932 marriage to Elfrida Howard was annulled upon discovery that he was (in the eyes of the law) a woman. Barker's contemporaries Mark Woods (reported in 1933) and Mark Weston (reported 1936) are interesting because they contain hints that reporters of the time perhaps had difficulty distinguishing between the signs of what might be gender reassignment vs intersex cases. This points to one of the first problems of dealing with historical evidence of cases that were perhaps incompletely described. However, two cases from only ten years later are much better documented: that of Dr Michael Dillon (see earlier), who left us an autobiography covering his surgeries and document changes in the early 1940s and another noble heir, Sir Ewan Forbes-Sempill of Craigievar (1912–1991), whose gender and official status change (enabling him to inherit the family baronetcy) was kept fairly quiet for many years and is now the subject of an entire book by Zoë Playdon. This, of course, raises a second bone of contention.

We have, by this point, two awkward challenges. The first is the question of whether some of the cases thrown up by historical digging are perhaps intersex rather than what you might term 'classically' trans or non-binary. The second is one of motive: are some cases really about women who, constrained by the limitations on their sex at the time, may have gone to all the trouble of changing their gender presentation so as to go to war, qualify as doctors, inherit property, marry another woman or whatever other limitation that might beset them?

In some cases, a study of behaviour provides the answer. Jazz musician Billy Tipton (1914–1989) not only lived as a man for most of his adult life (being 'revealed' only after his death) but also married and convinced his wife that he was a man. This was throughout a period in history when, although there was no civil partnership or same-sex marriage, few eyebrows were raised by two women choosing to live together as 'sisters'.

Perhaps the most contested case is that of Dr James Barry (1789–1865), covered in this book and often claimed as a feminist icon in the belief that they went to all the trouble to present most of their life as a man (a pretty misogynist one, at that) just so as to qualify and practise as a doctor and surgeon. You can see the appeal in that hypothesis. However, I'm intrigued more by the accounts of Barry's relationships with women and the trouble he took to insist that nobody should see him naked after death. That sounds much more 'trans man' to me. It's also interesting to compare Barry with a contemporary, Harry Stokes (1799–1859). Stokes worked for several decades in Manchester and Salford as a bricklayer. He had two marriages with women, but his female genital anatomy only came to official note after 40 years when, following his drowning in the River Irwell, questions were raised at the inquest into his death. It is said that working-class locals either knew or suspected Stokes' 'secret' but were content to let it lie. Similarly, James Barry was evidently helped – imagine the trouble (long before cross-sex hormones) of regularly concealing such a dramatic bodily function as monthly menstruation.

But there is, in fact, quite a rich history of gender crossing both ways in the 18th and 19th centuries, as this book illustrates brilliantly with more names than I've ever encountered before. Even more delightful are the personalities featured and beautifully illustrated from even further back. See, for instance, Moll Cutpurse (1584–1659), Francisco de Loyola (1585–1650), Marguerite Malaure (b. 1665), and Mark Read (1685 or 1690–1721), who were all being quite outrageous gender outlaws through a turbulent period of history.

When I read about early 20th century figures like Dora Richter or Lily Elbe, both born around 1890, I tend to compare them with my own grandparents, born that same decade and alive in my youth. That makes them people I can imagine, had they lived just another 30 years. Similarly with Christine Jorgensen, Roberta Cowell, Dr Michael Dillon and Ewan Forbes-Sempill, I am looking at contemporaries of my parents. That makes all these people more relatable to me and less like just names in a book. Depending on your age, you might try similar comparisons. It's harder perhaps to relate to people from earlier – Moll Cutpurse would have been marauding when my 11th great grandparents were alive, at the time of the Stuarts and into the English Civil War. To understand their lives better (and answer those vexing questions of how they connect to modern gender variant people) we all probably need to study more history, particularly what it was like to be an ordinary working-class person. Nevertheless, this book provides so many character sketches and visualizations that it is a start.

You may dispute whether trans, non-binary or intersex people can claim some of these characters. That's an invitation to more study, and maybe some of them will be better understood as a result. Meanwhile, I commend to you to the contribution made by this fascinating book.

Christine Burns MBE

Editor, *Trans Britain: Our Journey from the Shadows*

Introduction

It is so important that we know our shared history.

We see ourselves, in part, through the depiction of others' earlier lives and create our own identities based on those who came before us. This book should be an opportunity for the young and the old to see themselves mirrored in some of the lives and people included, or even to see this as a sourcebook of possibilities. I hope it will go some way to making everyone proud of who we all are.

An aim of the book is to produce evidence of the range of gender non-conforming presentations that have been possible throughout history. Some in early cultures and religions were even castrated, such as the hijras in India. Now the modern movements have given more voice to those who reject surgical interventions and the medicalization of transgender and intersex people. There are estimates that two thirds of transgender people of both sexes in the UK haven't gone through sex reassignment surgery for different reasons. However, some of our most important allies have been those who pioneered gender reassignment surgeries, like Dr Magnus Hirschfeld, Dr Harold Gillies and Dr Georges Burou. They link several pioneers.

Many self-identified by choosing to present as a different, preferred gender. More recently, some define themselves as non-binary. Those who cross-dressed also added to the awareness of transgender, non-binary and intersex people. For example, Missy, an aristocrat and French author Colette's partner, was prevented from buying a house dressed as a man. Visionary Joan of Arc broke parole by returning to dress as a man. The gender identities of landowner Gentleman Jack/Anne Lister (included in this book), Spanish soldier Francisco de Loyola/Catalina de Erauso (included in this book) and other early figures are still debated. It seems that how they are defined has as much to do with the concerns of the researchers and writers as with the history of the individual. They were brave individuals who existed before the science of gender reassignment surgery was developed.

Men passed as women, like performing duo Lady Stella Clinton and Miss Fanny Winifred Park (included in this book). Some worked as prostitutes, using Molly houses. These, with Mother Clap's being the most famous, existed from the 18th century. In 1880, the Manchester City Police raided what was called a fancy-dress ball at the Temperance Hall in York Street, Hulme in Manchester. Half the attendees at this very early example of a drag ball were cross-dressing men. In more modern times, trans women like Fulvia Sandoval, Alexis Arquette, Cristina Ortiz Rodríguez, Coccinelle, Jackie Shane and countless more had flourishing careers in the entertainment industries of their countries.

Women usually passed as male in order to access the privileges of men: money, work, travel, adventure, or even for religious purposes. Individuals like Moll Cutpurse and Mark Read were very adventurous, but many would have blended in more covertly. From the English Civil War to World War I, many women passing as men went to war, like the English Hannah Snell and American Albert D. J. Cashier. A traditional folk song in the UK and USA is 'Sweet Polly Oliver', which uses the name given to these cross-dressing women. It details the story of Polly, who joined the army disguised as her brother. Benjamin Britten arranged the UK version and Shirley Collins sings the USA version on her 2016 album *Lodestar*.

The prospect of self-identification is fought against by those believing in heteronormative ideology. In the UK, those with heteronormative views fought to limit the 2021 census and to stop the reform of the Gender Recognition Act, and more. But they don't realize that gender diversity has been a constant for millennia. It is only relatively recently that any official permissions have been available and/or required to adopt different genders and only in the last few decades that complete medical interventions have been provided (if with very long waiting times of between 12 and 32 months at gender identity clinics (GICs)). Yet, it can still take determination to present yourself as you know you should when others may take it as a confrontation and a challenge.

One change that would make a difference to all societies is for them to get rid of the myth of the binary. Even biologically it makes no sense, as nature is never so neat. There are over eight million possible variations in the genetic information inherited from parents in the 23 pairs of chromosomes. Differences to the XX = female and XY = male arrangement of the sex chromosomes usually involves extra ones being included with the pair, so that an infant may be born with three, four or five sex chromosomes (such as XYY, XXXY, XXXXY, etc.).

Beyond that, the number of gender variations can vary enormously, depending on the source. The Queensland Institute of Technology conducted an Australian sex survey in 2020 that listed 33 options for expressions of gender. Healthline.com produced a medically reviewed list of 64 terms to describe gender expression and identity and, helpfully, also included a list of 46 terms describing sexual orientation and behaviour. But I have seen lists of more than a hundred. The initials LGBT have expanded to LGBTQQIP2SAA (standing for lesbian, gay, bisexual, transgender, questioning, queer, intersex, pansexual, Two-Spirit, androgynous and asexual).

But even this list doesn't cover everyone. Writer and theorist Paul B. Preciado defines himself as countersexual. Musician and artist Genesis P-Orridge counted themselves as third gender and in a pandrogeny project with musician and artist Lady Jaye. Nor does it include those who define as just genderqueer. Androgyny can refer to the biology of intersex people, but also includes other ambiguous expressions of gender and sex in fashion or behaviour. Neutrois is a related name, but primarily used to define a person who has no gender or wants to limit expressions of their gender.

Writer and activist Leslie Feinberg included bi-gender in our community and used the term (in the book *Transgender Warriors*) to include anyone with combined female and masculine traits, or who is either cross-gender or a cross-dresser. Feinberg preferred these terms to transvestite, but includes drag queens and drag kings amongst those who also challenge the gender stereotypes (which are, after all, primarily a religious and/or Western construct). Professor Jack Halberstam has also debated the intersection between butch lesbians and female to male (FTM) trans people.

We do have a fluid attitude to gender and that doesn't always stop. For example, artist and actor Chella Man still identifies as trans-masculine, but now uses they/them. Activist and writer Kate Bornstein, one of my heroines, is trans-feminine, but also now uses they/them. I have tried to be careful about the use of pronouns, but I do apologize if I have made a mistake, or if there is an individual error in the text.

I have used he/him/his, she/her/hers and they/them/their pronouns. French and German people have du or sie, tu or vous. As I write this in April 2021, Spain's parliament and academy are still debating about rewriting their constitution to make it gender neutral. 'Ellos' is a criticized gender-inclusive pronoun, and 'elle' is more favoured. The conservative opposition put forward the old argument that the masculine form – mankind – is itself gender neutral and the feminine form only needs to be used if that particular sex has to be designated. We need either more pronouns for all the different possible genders or just a single one for everybody. Some languages, like Vietnamese, have the same pronoun for all uses of third person singular.

Members of cultures that uphold traditional transgender expression should be better known. Feinberg, again, refers to other cultural and traditional trans societies, which have also existed for all history and on every continent: the Basaja of Sulawesi, the Korean Mudang, the ancient Chinese Shih-Niang, the Lugbara in Africa name male to female (MTF) as Okule and FTM as Agule. Both groups are named Isangoma by the Zulu. Other native tribes in Africa, America and the Arctic have all traditionally supported cross-gender members of their communities. With all the evidence gathered and presented in this book and with more available, our presence and our diversity from antiquity to the present day should be acknowledged. What surprises me is how often being LGBTQI+ seems to be thought of as a recent phenomenon, such as the case of some Russians (and neighbouring illiberal regimes) repeating the gay propaganda myth, that homosexuality is a ploy of the Western powers to destroy their countries.

In fact, ancient Russia tolerated it when Europe didn't. Then, in the 17th century, Tsar Alexis introduced the death penalty for male and female homosexuality and Tsar Peter the Great criminalized it in the armed forces. However, a queer culture thrived. The Tsarist prohibitions were overturned by the more progressive revolutionaries in 1917. Stalin then imposed new anti-gay laws in 1933, which were again removed after his death, and homosexuality was decriminalized in 1993. Putin reimposed its criminalization again in 2013, presenting it as being 'against the norm of society and a contradiction to traditional family values'. The current laws now make the distribution of 'propaganda of non-traditional sexual relationships' among minors an offence. This definition includes material that 'raises interest' in such relationships, causes minors to 'form non-traditional sexual predispositions' or 'present distorted ideas about the equal social value of traditional and non-traditional sexual relationships'.[1] The vagueness of the language deliberately and dangerously leaves considerable room for interpretation.

It is reminiscent of the Section 28 legislation that Margaret Thatcher and her Tory government introduced earlier in the UK in 1988. It prohibited local authorities from 'promoting' homosexuality or gay 'pretended family relationships', and using educational materials and

---

1   Human Rights Watch (2018, December 11) 'No support: Russia's "gay propaganda law imperils LGBT youth".' Accessed on 11/09/2021 at www.hrw.org/report/2018/12/12/no-support/russias-gay-propaganda-law-imperils-lgbt-youth
    Pink News (2013, June 30) Russia: Putin signs anti-"gay propaganda" bill into law.' Accessed on 11/09/2021 at www.pinknews.co.uk/2013/06/30/russia-putin-signs-anti-gay-propaganda-bill-into-law

projects perceived to promote a gay lifestyle. Again, the language was deliberately vague and open to interpretation, so any discussion about LGBTQI+ issues was effectively banned. In the event it was repealed in 2003, but it had stifled virtually all debate in schools.

The terms 'Male, Female and Other' are used by the government (and in surveys, forms and questionnaires). Hopefully they will soon be replaced by something more inclusive. There is no reason that official and other documents and forms cannot include the different presentations that reflect the diversity and fluidity of genders of the modern world. The non-gendered activist Christie Elan-Cane has fought for a gender-neutral passport option in the UK for many years. It is important for the 600,000+ people in Britain who don't present as male or female and also for those who are transitioning.

The International Civil Aviation Organization recognizes all machine-readable passports with an X gender marker. These are issued by Australia, Austria, Canada, Denmark, Germany, Iceland, India, Malta, Netherlands, New Zealand, Nepal, Pakistan and Uruguay. All are recognized in the UK. The USA is following by issuing passports with the non-binary X gender marker.

In writing this book, I have spent time with many historical figures, all of whom have a unique story to share. It has been fascinating for me to discover these important figures, with the discovery of one leading to the discovery of many more. I hope you connect with their stories. Do take this as a call out for others' names that I have been unable to include, or have missed – please email me with your suggestions and discoveries.

phildpunchard@hotmail.co.uk

Alan L. Hart
(1890–1962)

Alan grew up preferring to be male and dressed as a boy from the age of five. He fell in love with female teachers at school, where he was forced to present as female. At college, Alan started an affair with an Eva Cushman and paid the fees for her to go with him to Albany College in Oregon. Alan also started cross-dressing and had affairs with other women. One of those paid for his fees to attend medical school. He graduated with the highest honours but was unhappy that the degree carried his female name and that this would prevent him being hired as the male he was.

He consulted Dr Joshua Allen Gilbert about continuing to live as a man. It does seem that Alan knew of Karl M. Baer's transition and the publications from Dr Magnus Hirschfeld about his work with Karl. Alan later adopted his mother's maiden name, Bamford, which he had preferred to use at college, and married a teacher, Inez Stark, in California early in 1918. Later in that same year, Dr Gilbert acceded to Alan's request and performed a hysterectomy to stop him menstruating. It was the only gender reassignment available to him. He legally changed his name and identified as male for the rest of his life. He kept the prior identity from before his transition a secret. Alan started taking hormones as soon as they were manufactured in 1920.

He lost two hospital positions after being identified as transgender. Inez and he divorced in 1925, and Alan married Edna Ruddick, a teacher like Inez, and they remained married until he died in 1962. As a result of the testosterone Alan began taking when it was manufactured after World War I, he started growing a beard and developed a deeper voice.

He earned a master's degree in radiology in 1930 and another in public health in 1948. He became an expert on tuberculosis, X-rays and radiation treatment and also wrote a number of novels.

Albert D. J. Cashier
(1843–1915)

There are different interpretations of the pronouns that should be used for the illiterate Albert Cashier, so I will use the neutral they/them. They were born female in Ireland and travelled to America as a teenager, probably dressing as a man already. They were able to join the 95th Illinois Volunteer Infantry on its formation in 1862 dressed as recruit Albert Cashier. They were able to wash and sleep separately and maintain the identity of a male soldier. Women did dress as men to earn better wages in jobs not normally available to them in the 1800s. There are over 400 documented cases of women known to have fought as men (called 'Polly Olivers') in the Civil War, including the Confederate spy and lieutenant Harry T. Buford. Another served, died and was buried as Private Lyons Wakeman, but many would have been uncounted.

In 1863, during the Siege of Vicksburg in Mississippi, Albert was captured, but they attacked a guard and escaped. Another reported incident was Albert braving the enemy shots and attaching the company's flag to a branch of a tree. Albert also fought in Missouri and Tennessee, withstanding many marches and fighting in 40 engagements during which nearly 300 men died. They were accepted as one of the men and as a good and brave soldier. In 1865, after the war and serving for the full enlistment period of three years, Albert joined the other soldiers back in civilian life. They added to an army pension by doing labouring work and other odd jobs. As shown, they continued dressing as a man. Though their true gender was, apparently, discovered by some, they kept the secret.

In 1911, after being hit by a senator's car, the senator (or a sympathetic doctor) helped them into a soldiers' home in Illinois without disclosing that Albert was female. There, Albert could share memories of the Civil War with the other veterans. In 1914, suffering from a form of dementia, they were taken to a psychiatric hospital and put into female dress (which may have caused a fall that broke their hip). They died after a rapid decline at the age of 71. Albert was respected by his army comrades and was given a full military funeral and buried in uniform. The headstone fellow soldiers put up had the name Albert D. J. Cashier on it. In 1977, a second headstone was put up, which, oddly, also included the name that Albert had rejected (literally dead-naming him).

Woman Soldier in 95th Ill.

ALBERT D. J. CASHIER
OF
COMPANY G, 95TH ILLINOIS REGIMENT

Photographed November, 1864

ALBERT D. J. CASHIER
OF
COMPANY G, 95TH ILLINOIS REGIMENT

Photographed July, 1913

Anne Lister *aka* Gentleman Jack (1791–1840)

(I will use Lister's surname to avoid the confusion of Anne and her partner, Ann.)

Lister's appearance was unapologetically manly, and she planned to always wear black, which was why her neighbours nicknamed her Gentleman Jack. She has been called 'the first modern lesbian', which ignores the notable 'Ladies of Llangollen' who predated her slightly, and Lister did visit them. She was certainly gender fluid and can be considered as transgender as it was possible to be in her time. Her home, Shibden Hall in Halifax, is popular with Lister's admirers and general tourists. It inspired playwright Sally Wainwright, who has visited it since childhood.

Her 26 volumes of diaries that, fortunately, survive contain valuable insights into 19th century life. But it is the large, encoded sexual content of the diaries that fascinates modern readers. The diaries are now part of a UNESCO programme and used in gender and women's studies. An edited version and biographies are currently available. Lister started her first lesbian affair at 13 with Eliza Raine, with whom she shared a bedroom at their York school, before Lister was expelled. Lister first started using her codes for secret messages to Raine. She inherited Shibden Hall, the home of her childless aunt and uncle, in 1823. She lived there from 1815, which was after all four of her brothers had died.

In 1834, after having had many lovers, Lister and Ann Walker celebrated a marriage by sharing communion at Holy Trinity Church in York (which now has a blue plaque with the LGBTQI+ rainbow edging to celebrate the event). Lister's diaries (digitized with Wainwright's help) also detail her many successful business dealings and the improvements she made to Shibden Hall. There are 14 travel notebooks that describe the many journeys that she made from the age of 28. They were extensive and include most of Europe and the UK. A honeymoon trip with Ann Walker included an early ascent of the Vignemale peak in the French Pyrenees (a 17-hour round trip). On a last trip with Walker, in 1839, they went to Russia and then travelled south to Georgia, where Lister contracted a fever and died. Her embalmed body was then buried inside her parish church but was only rediscovered in 2010.

Barbette *aka* Vander Clyde Broadway (1898–1973)

Barbette was a trapeze artist, who achieved iconic status in the 1920s and 1930s, particularly in France, as the copy of the Gesmar poster demonstrates. Barbette gained considerable following amongst the intelligentsia and avant-garde. Effectively, audiences were applauding a male to female (MTF) performer. By the age of 14, Barbette was in full drag as one of The Alfaretta Sisters' aerialist act in American circuses. By 1919, Barbette was a solo female high wire and trapeze act in vaudeville theatres, revealing a male identity when he had finished. In 1923, Barbette appeared in Europe. At the London Palladium she was caught having sex with a man and was never able to get an English work permit again.

Jean Cocteau wrote to Paul Collaer in 1923, '...tell everybody that he is no mere acrobat in women's clothes, nor just a graceful daredevil, but one of the most beautiful things in the theatre. Stravinsky, Auric, poets, painters and I myself have seen no comparable display of artistry on the stage since Nijinsky.' He also called Barbette 'an angel, a flower, a bird'. And in 1926 he wrote an essay[2] about Barbette about how she '...plays the part of a man' at the end of the act. Cocteau had a short affair with Barbette and got Man Ray to produce a series of photographs of the transformation into Barbette. He also cast her in his film, *Le Sang d'un poète*. Hitchcock's film *Murder!* has a 'Barbette' in it, and the 1933 German film *Viktor und Viktoria* used Barbette's signature reveal.

In the late 1930s, Barbette had to cease performing, most likely due to the effects of a fall and subsequent surgery. Despite continuing pain, Barbette then worked as a trainer and consultant for other acts and for theatrical productions and films. He worked with Orson Welles on *Around the World with Orson Welles* and films such as *Till the Clouds Roll By* and *The Big Circus*, as well as coaching Jack Lemmon and Tony Curtis for *Some Like It Hot*. In 1961, Barbette appeared in the director Curtis Harrington's impressive debut feature *Night Tide*, which also had Dennis Hopper's first starring role. A *New Yorker* article in 1969 about Barbette was entitled 'An Angel, a Flower, a Bird'. Barbette died from an overdose.

---

2   'La Numéro Barbette' published in the journal Nouvelle Revue Française.

Betty Cooper *aka* Cato (mid-18th century)

Middle of picture

A fascinating facet of 18th century cross-dressing and trans lives is that involving escaping slaves. Betty Cooper was one of them, and the main evidence of her existence is a short notice from her owner in a Boston newspaper:

> Ran away from his Master John Sober, Esq; on Monday the 8th of April Inst. A Negro Man Servant, named Cato, formerly owned by Mr. William Cooper of Boston, and well known by the Name of Miss Betty Cooper; – Whoever takes up said Negro, and will bring him to the Subscriber shall have TWELVE DOLLARS Reward, and all necessary Charges Paid. JOHN SOBER, Boston, April 12, 1771

Historians have suggested that she was well known as an early drag queen and noted that owners weren't always concerned with slaves' sexualities and gender boundaries that may have been brought from the non-binary traditions of their own cultures. The former owner, Cooper, was the town clerk, which may have also made Betty known to many. In pre-revolutionary America, there were no safe states for slaves to flee to and there was some evidence that Betty went to Georgia from Boston, a reversal of the expected journey.

Ellen Craft (1826–1891) *and* William Craft (1824–1900)

Top left and right of picture

Ellen and William Craft escaped from enslavement in Georgia in December 1848 and arrived in Philadelphia on Christmas Day by travelling first class on steamboat and train. Their daring ploy was for Ellen to masquerade as a white, male slave owner, pretending to have an injured arm to avoid having to write, with William as his servant. Their daring had been publicized and celebrated by abolitionists. Unfortunately, whilst living in Boston, the 1850 Fugitive Slave Act threatened their freedom by requiring free states to return slaves to their owners. They escaped again to England and finally to 26 Cambridge Grove, Hammersmith, in London and had five children (where a blue plaque was put up in 2021). After the end of the Civil War, they returned to America and set up a school for the children of freed slaves.

Biawacheeitchish (Woman Chief) *aka* Pine Leaf (1806–1858)

Kidnapped as a ten-year-old child by a Native American Crow tribe from the Gros Ventres people, Pine Leaf was adopted by a warrior whose two sons had been killed. He encouraged their interest in male activities like horse riding and marksmanship. They grew up as a gender variant Two-Spirit and took over the foster father's role after his death, whilst still wearing female clothes. They led successful raiding parties against Blackfoot settlements. Those deeds were rewarded by an elevation to the council of chiefs and being given the name Biawacheeitchish, which means Woman Chief in English. They remained a fierce warrior and were the tribe's war chief for 20 years, becoming third in ranking of the 160 lodge chiefs. They gained wealth and prestige and took four wives. Before being killed in a Gros Ventres raid, Biawacheeitchish had negotiated many peace treaties.

Other warrior women in the Crow nation include Akkeekaahuush (c.1810–1880) and another war leader, Biliíche Héeleelash (c.1837–1912), and Osh-Tisch remains famous as last of the Crow baté. Interestingly, the Cheyenne Buffalo Calf Road Woman fought at the Battle of the Little Bighorn and is reputed to have knocked Custer off his horse. The Sioux, Thašína Máni and the Lakota One Who Walks With the Stars were also at the battle.

Native American tribes (also known as First Nations and Indigenous People) have, historically, adopted a looser idea of gender. They had four classifications – feminine woman, masculine woman, feminine man and masculine man – rather than the binary choice. Two-Spirit is actually a modern English-language term devised at a Native American LGBTQI+ meeting at Winnipeg in 1990 and has never been universally approved among the tribes. Its purpose was to differentiate themselves from the modern binary terminology, but it has been criticized for not considering the spiritual and ceremonial roles of the entire four genders.

Bill Allen
(1906–1949)

Bill's story isn't pleasant, and it was described in great detail by the newspapers. He was the last transgender person to be hanged (and maybe the first?). He was assigned female at birth, one of 22 children in a Catholic family. But he presented as male from childhood and was accepted by most of his neighbours as such. He earned his living in physically demanding jobs in the Lancashire cotton mills. He also worked as a labourer and postman and was a bus conductor in the 1940s. He copied the rough language and behaviour of the men he worked and drank in the pubs with. After his mother died in 1943, his behaviour worsened, his appearance deteriorated, he drank more and he suffered from periods of depression. He attempted to gas himself a number of times. In 1946, he was sacked by the bus company he worked for for swearing at and being abusive to passengers and did little work after that.

In August 1948, he beat to death his 68-year-old neighbour, Nancy Chadwick, after she had come to borrow some sugar. He used a coal hammer on her because, he claimed, he was 'in one of my funny moods'.[3] She was reputed to be a miser, who carried a lot with her (and Bill was jobless and in debt). Her body was left outside Bill's house, and bloodstains, which he hadn't bothered cleaning up, led from the street into his home. One argument that his defence used was that he must be insane because he cross-dressed. That failed to influence the jury, who, after a short trial and a 15-minute consideration, declared him guilty. He was hanged in January 1949 at Strangeways Prison. The hangman was the 'celebrated' public executioner, Albert Pierrepoint.

Some describe Bill as gender confused, or say that he was a cross-dressing lesbian. He claimed that a period he spent in hospital in 1935 was to have an operation to become a man, though that was very unlikely to be possible for him at that time. He did definitely think of himself as male, and there seems no doubt that he would now be defined as transgender. He did have a girlfriend, Annie Cook, but she rejected his attempts to have sex with her. Bill continued to be difficult and aggressive in the death cell, shouting and arguing with the prison officers. This continued to the end, and he threw his last meal at the wall (he had chosen scrambled eggs). A convention at the execution was to grant the condemned person time for a last statement, but Bill rejected that opportunity.

---

3   Murderpedia (n.d.) 'Margaret Allen.' Accessed on 09/11/2021 at https://murderpedia.org/female.A/a/allen-margaret.htm

Brandon Teena
(1972–1993)

Brandon was murdered, and his short life was subject to a number of reinterpretations in news reports, articles, books and films. Like much earlier people, he was reported to have 'posed' as male and was also called a lesbian. His killers were John Lotter and Marvin Tom Nissen, who also killed two witnesses, Phillip DeVine and Lisa Lambert. Lotter was given a death sentence, but Nissen gave evidence against Lotter and was given three life sentences.

Brandon reported to the police that he had been beaten and raped by John Lotter and Tom Nissen on Christmas Eve 1993, six days before they killed him. No action was taken against the rapists despite the interrogation of Brandon by police sheriff Charles Laux. His mother, JoAnn Brandon, later successfully sued the police, with the judge stating that the questioning that Brandon was subjected to was intimidating, demeaning and accusatory. (The 1998 documentary, *The Brandon Teena Story*, details this humiliating experience.) After finding out that Brandon had reported them, the killers tracked him to Lisa Lambert's house, where they shot Brandon, Lisa and Phillip. It was New Year's Eve. Lisa's little son wasn't harmed.

Brandon and his elder sister were brought up by their widowed mother in a mobile home and were both subject to rape and sexual abuse by their uncle. It was in his adolescence that Brandon began identifying as male. As a teenager, he used chest bindings and also began dating girls. His gender dysphoria led to him being expelled from school just prior to graduation, and he also tried to enlist in the army as male. In 1992, he was assessed and given treatment for a 'sexual identity crisis'. It was shortly after this that he moved to Falls City, Nebraska, in his male identity and begun dating Lana Tisdel, a friend of Lisa's, and meeting Phillip and the killers. He told Lisa that he was intersex and aiming to have sex reassignment surgery.

Hilary Swank played Brandon in the 1999 film *Boys Don't Cry*. Lana successfully sued the filmmakers for their portrayal of her and Brandon's mother, and even criticized Hilary for referring to Brandon as male in her Oscar acceptance speech.

Carlett Angianlee Brown
(b. circa 1927)

Carlett was a 1950s 'shake dancer'; shake dancing was a wild and uninhibited kind of dancing. Most of her story appeared in several issues of *Jet* magazine, which followed her transition in, sometimes critical, articles in 1953. She had been unthinkingly assigned as male when she was born. In 1950, she joined the US Navy and consulted their doctors about the monthly bleeding from her rectum. She was diagnosed as intersex, with some female internal organs. Rather than agreeing for them to be removed, she decided that she wanted to become the first African American to have sex reassignment surgery (SRS) (although that honour may have later been won by Delisa Newton as late as 1965). She had plans to also have facial feminization surgery (using blues singer Tamara Hayes' features as a guide). She also wanted to marry Eugene Martin, a 24-year-old US Army sergeant based in Germany once she had the SRS done. She performed in Boston after leaving the Navy and while arranging her transition.

Since Christine Jorgensen (the first widely known individual in the US to have SRS), no US citizen was allowed to alter their sex in America and none of the European surgeons that Carlett investigated was allowed to provide SRS for an American in their countries. She was given the options of applying to become a German citizen and having it done there or relinquishing her US citizenship and having it done by the Danish surgeon (Dr Christian Hamburger), who had previously treated Christine Jorgensen in 1952. She chose the latter and took the first steps in arranging her travel at a Danish consulate. She got her new passport in the name of Carlett Angianlee Brown, despite having been arrested again for cross-dressing. She decided to have the facial surgery first with Dr George Weiss in New York for $500, but then had a tax demand for back taxes of $1200. Carlett had to work as a cook to pay off her tax debt. There are no further details of Carlett from any source, but it seems unlikely that she was, ultimately, able to get the surgeries she had wanted, or that news would have been given. Other African American trans women of this period were Ava Betty Brown, Lucy Hicks Anderson, Georgia Black and others.

Charles Hamilton
(circa 1721–1770)

Charles reportedly began dressing as a boy at 14. He assisted unlicensed (quack) doctors, before setting himself up as one at Wells in Somerset in 1746. A little later in the same year, he married his landlady's daughter, Mary Price. She helped Charles with his business and reportedly believed that they had sex (which, in a contemporary newspaper report, was 'owing to [Charles] using certain vile and deceitful practices, not fit to be mentioned'). However, Mary did eventually discover that Charles was female and reported him, which led to his arrest and trial in Taunton. As with some later examples of 'female husbands', the general attitude was that cross-dressers were deceivers and cheats. During his trial, there were rumours that Charles had married several women, and the prosecutor in the trial also claimed that Charles had contracted 14 marriages.

The verdict was guilty, and he was sentenced to six months' imprisonment. He was also to be publicly whipped in Taunton, Glastonbury, Wells and Shepton Mallet. However, despite all the exaggerated outrage that was expressed during the trial and in the reporting of it, Charles was only convicted of a 'fraudulent marriage'.

The case, as one of the earliest (if not the very earliest) of its kind, attracted the attention of the author Henry Fielding (the author of *The History of Tom Jones, a Foundling* and many other novels and plays). At the end of 1746, he published anonymously a 23-page pamphlet, *The Female Husband or the Surprising History of Mrs Mary alias Mr George Hamilton*. His version of Charles' biographical details and the consequent events differ from the actual ones quite significantly. His Hamilton was led astray by her friend, Anne Johnson, and 'vile amours... transactions not fit to be mention'd passed between them'.[4] According to Fielding, that precedent set his Hamilton on his path of crime, marrying many women for money. Interestingly, Fielding varied the gender pronouns that he used for his Hamilton.

In 1752, a Pennsylvanian newspaper reported the discovery of a cross-dressing itinerant doctor called Charles Hamilton. Fielding died in 1754, but an amended version of his titillating story was published in 1813 with the engraving of the whipping. Comedian, actor and writer Sandi Toksvig starred in a 2006 BBC radio play by Sheila Hannon that was based on the later version of Fielding's story.

---

4   Fielding, H. (2007) *The History of Tom Jones: and The Female Husband*. London: Vintage, p.863.

Chevalier d'Éon
(1728–1810)

Charles-Geneviève-Louis-Auguste-André-Timothée d'Éon de Beaumont was born in Burgundy. I will use they/them pronouns because there some evidence that d'Éon was intersex. They said that they were female at birth, though the father presented his child to the world as male in order to gain an inheritance. D'Éon continued as a male soldier for nearly 50 years. However, there are accounts of d'Éon also identifying as a woman during this time, including an account that they spied on the Russian court of Empress Elizabeth as a woman. They did serve as a captain in the French Army during the Seven Years' War and were wounded. They were later sent to London and drafted the peace treaty between the English and French.

D'Éon was given a pension and the title of Chevalier by Louis XVI in 1775 for their contributions to the peace negotiations (and after threatening to reveal secret information). The terms of the pension obliged d'Éon to remain in female dress. They returned to England and became a celebrated figure in society, performing fencing demonstrations, fighting duels and attending balls, all as a woman. There was even a court trial that settled d'Éon's status as a woman, and they were admired as such by Mary Wollstonecraft.

The French Revolution in 1789 brought all pension payments to an end, but d'Éon pledged to lead an army of women to help the revolution. In a copy of a 1792 painting of d'Éon that resides in the National Portrait Gallery, they are dressed as a supporter of the French Revolution. D'Éon is honoured as the first transsexual in the UK, and Havelock Ellis created the term 'Eonism' to describe trans behaviour. The transgender self-help organization is named the Beaumont Society after them. There is a memorial to them in the graveyard of St Pancras Old Church erected by Baroness Angela Georgina Burdett-Coutts. They lived with their governess for 50 years but married at 67 after her death. They lived until they were 82.

Christine Jorgensen
(1926–1989)

Christine was born in the Bronx and named after her Danish father. She has said that she was always feminine and that gays rejected her for being too 'cissy'. She did explain that her chromosomes were XXXY (instead of the normal XY for males or XX for females). After service during World War II, she attempted to resolve her confused state of mind in the USA but rejected a psychiatrist's 'gay cure'. Instead, she started hormone treatment with the help of a Dr Joseph Angelo, the husband of a friend.

Jorgensen researched transsexuality and the relevant operations. There were few available, but there was advanced transsexual research in Denmark. She was treated by Dr Christian Hamburger between 1950 and 1952 as a research project. He prescribed more hormones and administered an orchiectomy and later a penectomy. She chose her name 'Christine' to honour him. Her vaginoplasty was completed later by the same Dr Angelo who had initially helped

her. Dr Harry Benjamin, a specialist in transsexuality, acted as medical adviser. Dr Benjamin had got his medical degree from the University of Tübingen and was a friend of Dr Magnus Hirschfeld.

The *New York Daily News* made her headline news at the end of 1952 under the banner, 'Ex-GI Becomes Blonde Beauty'. She used that to become a performer and singer, and later lectured, wrote books and did interviews, some still available online. Jorgensen had bravely got the surgery she needed when so little was available. She also used her knowledge and status to promote understanding of trans issues (unlike Roberta Cowell) even at the height of the Cold War and McCarthyism.

In one interview a few years before her death from cancer, she said that she had loved twice but not got engaged to either. Jorgensen continued to campaign for available treatment and acceptance until her death from cancer.

Claude Cahun *aka* Lucy Renee Mathilde Schwob (1894–1954)

Claude was born to an intellectual Jewish family in 1894. By the time they were four, their mother had been put in an asylum. They were educated in England to avoid the antisemitism they had been subjected to in a French school. They returned to study at the Sorbonne and met artist Suzanne Malherbe in 1909. The pair lived and worked together for nearly half a century until Claude died. At eighteen, they were jointly making the many photographic portraits of Claude, portraying them in many guises and disguises. In 1917, Suzanne's widowed mother married Claude's divorced father and the pair of (now) step-siblings changed their names. In France, the name Claude can be male or female, and Cahun was their grandmother's name. Suzanne became Marcel (which can also be a male or female name), with the adopted surname of Moore. Together they continued producing theatre, photography, poems and other artworks, which were inspired by the surrealist movement. They also collaborated with the Dadaist and Surrealist Man Ray and Georges Bataille, surrealist, philosopher, mystic and author of *Story of the Eye* (once thought pornographic).

In the autobiography *Disavowals: Or Cancelled Confessions*, Claude questioned how they could be defined as male or female when they preferred to be described as neuter. In 1937, the couple moved from Paris to Jersey. The Germans invaded in 1940 and the pair surreptitiously distributed anti-Nazi propaganda to the soldiers for nearly four years until they were both arrested and sentenced to death. The liberation of the island saved them, but their home and property had been confiscated and a lot of their art destroyed. By then Claude was in ill health and died a few years later. Marcel survived until dying by suicide. They are now both buried together at St Brelade's Church. Their shared artwork has been increasingly exhibited, sometimes alongside successors such as Gillian Wearing and Cindy Sherman. David Bowie included their work in a multi-media show in 2007 at New York's High Line Festival. In 2018, a street in the 6th arrondissement, near where they lived in Paris, was renamed after them and included the description: Couple d'artistes et de resistantes (Couple of artists and resistance fighters).

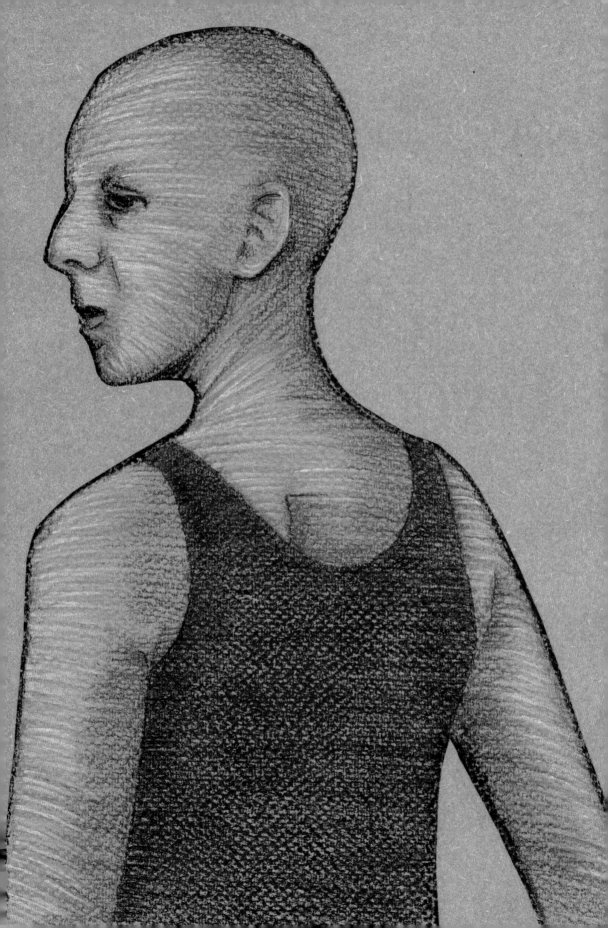

Colonel Victor Barker *aka* Valerie Arkell-Smith *and other names* (1895–1960)

Victor went by a number of names, some that signified a change of gender from female to male and others because he was a bankrupt and convicted criminal. He had a short marriage during World War I and, after driving ambulances in France, had another relationship and two children. By 1923, he had started another relationship, this time with a woman, Elfrida, whilst presenting as an injured serviceman (as a reason to keep elements of his physical appearance secret). The female to male (FTM) musician Billy Tipton used a similar reason; that he had been in a car crash that resulted in significant injury, therefore concealing elements of his physical appearance from those close to him. Victor and Elfrida later married, and he gave himself a knighthood before signing the marriage certificate (he deserted her in 1926 and faced a trial for providing incorrect information at the ceremony later).

In the mid 1920s, he had joined a fascist movement and became secretary to the leader, Henry Rippon Seymour, which he later excused as accidental. Though he went on 'red bashing' jaunts and helped train members in fighting, his gender seems never to have been questioned by them. In 1928, he was a bankrupt restaurant proprietor, and the court proceedings were completed with the defendant's name changed from male to female. He was then jailed in Holloway women's prison for contempt of court for non-appearance. A further sentence of nine months was added after his marriage was judged illegal, due to the false statements he made.

As I was born near Blackpool, I was interested in Victor's sideshow on the Blackpool promenade for 21 weeks in 1937. Conveniently, the Mass Observation Project visited the town in the same year, and Humphrey Spender photographed the entrance to the show. The hoarding read: 'I am taking this step for the woman I love – On a strange honeymoon – Love calling – Admission 2d'. Tom Harrison's *Britain Revisited* included the photograph and describes how the overweight Victor and his 'bride' were displayed. They were both on beds, separated by Belisha beacons, at the bottom of a pit. For 12 hours a day, they had to endure the comments shouted from the customers who walked round the top of the pit. There was also supposed to be a £250 bet that they wouldn't remain together during the 21 weeks (when more than a million people visited the sideshow). He then faded from the headlines, lived more quietly and died as Geoffrey Norton in Suffolk.

Dora (Dorchen) Richter
(1891–1933)

According to remaining records, Dora was the first trans woman to undergo gender reassignment surgery (vaginoplasty). It's reported that she tried to get rid of her penis when she was six years old. She cross-dressed from an early age and, as others, was arrested for doing that. In order to prevent these arrests, Dr Magnus Hirschfeld of the Berlin Institute for Sexual Research helped create transvestite passes with the cooperation of the police. Dora, also called Dorchen, worked at the institute as a female domestic servant. In 1922, she had an orchiectomy there and later a penectomy, with the vaginoplasty in 1931 performed by Dr Erwin Gohrbandt. In 1933, a Nazi mob attacked the institute, burnt its books and records and killed Dora and others.

In 1919, Dr Magnus Hirschfeld, with Richard Oswald, created the polemic film, *Different from the Others*. The story detailed the effects of homophobic legislation, blackmail and suicide. Dr Hirschfeld appeared as himself in the film, providing advice to Conrad Veidt's character, a gay musician, and to his friends. He also provided a summary of what he called 'The Third Sex', the physical causes for their valid sexuality and natural gender diversity. This section of the film showed the female Dora and her previous male persona as well as photographs of other unidentifiable patients of Dr Hirschfeld's clinic. Dr Hirschfeld stated his hopes that the German penal code's Paragraph 175 would be rescinded and that society would become more inclusive. In the event, the freedom to produce films such as this proved to be brief and tighter censorship was instituted within ten years. With the rise of fascism, the film was banned and all but destroyed. It still exists because of considerable restoration of the remaining parts and with the use of stills and intertitles.

Dr James Barry
(1789–1865)

Born Margaret Bulkley, Barry was the child of a Cork shopkeeper and, more importantly, the niece of artist James Barry. He used a bequest from his uncle to travel to Edinburgh and enrol at the school of medicine. Barry's slight figure and hairless chin forced him to pretend he was younger than he was, but that required some influence from Lord Buchan to enable the young graduate to collect his degree. Buchan also intervened when Barry had difficulty when he attempted to become an army surgeon.

Barry later spent 12 years in Cape Colony in South Africa, becoming the chief medical officer. Apparently, Barry used built-up shoes and some padding to appear more masculine. He also had a reputation for losing his temper easily, even fighting a duel.

Barry was a skilled surgeon and performed one of the first successful caesareans. He also enforced strict hygienic conditions in his hospitals and pressed for the improvement of the conditions for soldiers and prisoners in the colony.

He also served in the West Indies, the Mediterranean and Canada, becoming the inspector general for all military hospitals. After his death, Barry became the subject of gossip with regard to his gender identity and featured in a Charles Dickens article and play. Some have suggested he might have been intersex.

Whatever the debatable points are, Barry pursued his education, qualifications and military service long before any of them were available to women and was successful at all of them. Other transgender people existed in Britain, like Charles Hamilton, and were revealed, if at all, after many years of presenting as the opposite sex. They were sometimes put on trial, like Samuel Bundy (1759), Edward de Lacy Evans (1870s), Lois Schwich (1880s) and many more.

Dr John (Johann) Theodora de Verdion *aka* Miss Grahn (1744–1802)

There are conflicting versions of John's, or Johann's, life before he moved to London. One has him being born in Berlin and using an inheritance to set up as a broker there. Theodora adopted the name Baron de Verdion in Bayreuth in 1763 and was Johann Basedow's secretary until their close relationship attracted criticism and he fled to London. Another version has him born in Leipzig and as a man was employed in Bayreuth before his secret was discovered. Both accounts agree that he then travelled to London and advertised himself as John de Verdion, a teacher of German, French and English languages from his home in Hatton Garden. He taught German to Edward Gibbon (who wrote *The Decline and Fall of the Roman Empire*) and to William Cavendish-Bentinck, 3rd Duke of Portland, who was Prime Minister of Great Britain and then the UK. He appeared in etchings and books (like *Kirby's Wonderful and Eccentric Museum and Magazine of Remarkable Characters*). In many of them, she/her pronouns were used, despite de Verdion dressing as a man whilst living in London. *Kirby's* described his 'grotesque' appearance, but that seems to have been determined by them defining de Verdion as a woman.

The illustration contains the features that made him so recognizable: cocked hat, boots, cane and the umbrella that was always carried, along with the books, coins and medals bought at auctions to sell to dealers and acquaintances. He always visited Furnival's Inn and Coffee House for large meals, such as 'eighteen eggs and a proportionate quantity of bacon'. He was also reported to consume two bottles of wine at a sitting. After only once being helped home and put to bed, de Verdion insisted that, in future, he be left to sleep at Furnival's instead. Despite all de Verdion's endeavours, he appears not to have been very prosperous and suffered from nerves, perhaps because of the harassment and mockery he had to endure. He developed breast cancer and died at his lodgings in Upper Chase Street, Hatton Garden. The will, signed John de Verdion, left everything to Mr Denner, the owner of Furnival's. Unfortunately, there was little money left and it did not pay off the debt that had been allowed to develop. A coffin plate was made with the same name as the will but was then changed to read 'Miss de Verdion'.

Miss Grahn alias Theodora de Verdion.
A remarkable Walking Bookseller Quack Doctor &c &c

Stop Gentle Reader & Behold
A Beau in Boots, searching for Gold.
A Walking Bookseller, an Epicure.
A Teacher, Doctor & a Connoisseur.

Gratis — to the purchasers of the Wonderful Magazine ——— Pubd by C. Johnson

Elagabalus Marcus Aurelius Antonius Augustus

(203 or 204–222 CE)

Elagabalus was born at Emesa in Syria in a family of priests of the sun god Baal, whose local name Elah-Gabal formed the name of Elagabalus. Their father, Sextus Varius Marcellus, was a senator; their mother, Julia Soaemias, was a cousin of Emperor Caracalla; and their grandmother, Julia Maesa, was sister-in-law to Emperor Septimius Severus. Caracalla was murdered by Macrinus, but Elagabalus' mother made allies and Caracalla's forces were defeated. He and his family were killed, and Elagabalus was made the penultimate Roman emperor of the Severan dynasty at the age of 14, only to be killed four years later.

Contemporary accounts by Cassius Dio described Elagabalus' eccentric behaviour. They married five women but had many affairs with men found at public baths and elsewhere. One, Hierocles, became their husband, and some of them such as an athlete, Aurelius Zoticus, were given important offices of the state. Elagabalus also sought physicians who could give him female genitals. A castration wasn't carried through, but a circumcision was. Their whole body was depilated, and they wore silk dresses, embroidered in gold. They also had painted eyes and rouged cheeks and impersonated prostitutes, for which they liked to be punished by one of their lovers or members of the Praetorian Guard.

Yet, it was the flouting of laws and traditions that offended most. Elagabalus introduced the worship of Elah-Gabal/Baal and built a new temple on the Palatine Hill. The focus for the worship was a black meteorite that was brought from the temple in Emesa. Other sacred Roman relics were also included. Its entrance was flanked by two giant phalli, as it was a phallic-oriented cult. Elagabalus also raped and then married a Vestal Virgin in the sanctuary of Vesta in 220 CE, with the fruitless hope that their children would be god-like. Elagabalus' grandmother had been the power behind the throne, and she persuaded Elagabalus to adopt his nephew, Severus Alexander and appoint him as his heir. When Elagabalus was murdered, so was their mother and some of their favourites. Alexander was then made emperor. He was assassinated by his generals after 13 years of fighting invasions and destroying the economy.

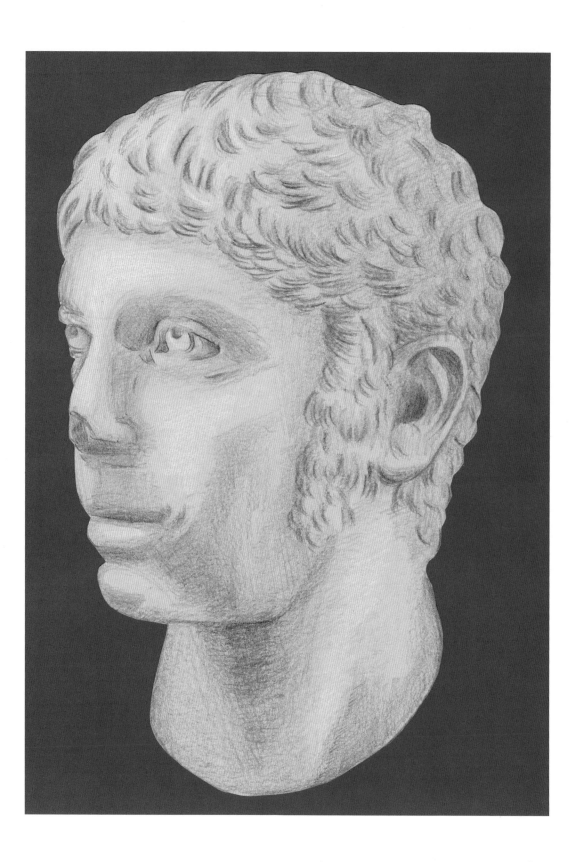

Francisco de Loyola *aka* Catalina/ Katalina de Erauso *and other names* (circa 1585–1650)

Francisco's father was a military commander and Francisco enjoyed joining in when his father and brothers practised their military skills. He was put into an aunt's convent in Basque, Spain, at the age of four and escaped from another (where he got into many fights and used to be locked away) when he was 15. He cut his hair, dressed in men's clothes and as Francisco de Loyola made his way to the royal court and became a page. He fled there after seeing his father and was imprisoned in Bilbao after injuring a man who had tried to assault him.

In 1608, after two years as a servant, he sailed to Mexico as a cabin boy. Whilst serving in the army, he courted women and fought duels until being sentenced to prison for two killings. After another escape he went to Peru but was jailed again after a knife fight. On release, Francisco enlisted in the army in Bolivia and fought the indigenous natives. He was imprisoned for another killing, but a rich widow helped him escape once more.

According to records, Francesco was the sole Spanish survivor of a sea battle against the Dutch off Peru in 1615. He then fought indigenous Chileans and was badly wounded but was made lieutenant for his bravery. He knifed another comrade and was later wounded in battle again. Then he captured a chieftain and hanged him. He was (again) the only survivor of three who crossed the Andes to get to Argentina. On returning to Peru, Francisco thought he had caught a fatal fever and confessed all to a priest. He became a celebrated figure and later left for Europe in 1623. He got a pension from the Spanish king and permission to dress as a man from Pope Urban VIII, but Pope Urban VIII told Francesco (reasonably) that he had to stop killing people. He wrote *The Ensign Nun*, before he returned to Mexico in 1635. He may have drowned at Veracruz, yet the bishop of Puebla reported that he had buried Francisco fifteen years later.

It's difficult to do justice to all Francesco's exploits. Many incidents may be apocryphal, and some are contradicted in different tellings of his life. There are also conflicting views on his sexual orientation and gender identity, as with many LGBTQI+ people of an earlier age. Though the pronouns used by others for Catalina are sometimes she/her, his memoir varies the possessive pronoun according to the gender he presented at different times.

George Sand *aka* Amantine Lucile Aurore Dupin (1804–1876)

A relevant feature of George's life is her cross-dressing and her reaction to the police order of 1800 that prohibited women choosing to wear male clothing in France. It was categorized as a dangerous practice to themselves and others. The order required the authorization of the prefecture of the police, a health official to declare that there was a medical necessity for male clothing and also signatures of other government officials. Without the authorized permit, the woman was, supposedly, likely to be arrested. George ignored it and just continued to wear men's clothes. The order wasn't rescinded until 2013. She also offended sensibilities further by smoking in public and frequenting venues that were usually barred to women. Contemporary Victor Hugo is cited as saying, '…it is not my place to decide whether she is my sister or my brother.'

George became more popular than writers Honoré de Balzac or Hugo. She was related to some European royal families on her father's side. She married Casimir Dudevant, who she said was a foolish drunkard. They had two children and developed an open marriage. She had many famous lovers like Gustave Flaubert, Prosper Mérimée, Alfred de Musset, and, most notably, Frédéric Chopin. Chopin was initially rude and asked the cross-dressing George if she was a man or woman, but they did have an affair. George probably had an affair with Marie Dorval, the actress, as well.

Her novels shocked some, and other writings, including manifestos, were politically radical and intended to further workers' and women's rights. She was a member of the provisional government after the French Revolution of 1848. She also published her own Republican newspaper with a workers' co-operative in 1848.

Napoleon III staged a coup d'état and later became de facto monarch of the Second French Empire. Many fellow Republicans fled or were arrested, but George remained and continued to fight the excesses of the new regime. Russian novelist Fyodor Dostoyevsky was a great admirer of hers, as were other authors as diverse as Walt Whitman, Marcel Proust, Virginia Woolf and others. At least five biopics have been made about her.

Harry Allen *aka* Harry Livingstone (1882–1922)

After giving birth to an illegitimate child at the age of 16, Harry passed the child to his grandparents and adopted his masculine and very boisterous lifestyle. He, reportedly, made a charming and handsome man who also liked to dress well. Within a few years (as Harry Livingstone) he had been arrested for cross-dressing a number of times in Seattle. He was featured in many newspaper articles until his death. One in the *Philadelphia Times* in May 1900 was headed 'A woman by nature – a man by choice'. Harry had many jobs: bartender, barber, wrangler, longshoreman, and he was a good musician. He kept getting in trouble, beginning in Tunnel City, Washington, which was named 'the wickedest place on earth' by the *St Paul Globe*, and Seattle wasn't much better. He lived in its districts where vice, corruption and crime were prevalent. He appears to have had many female lovers. Dolly Quappe killed herself by drinking carbolic acid, Pearl Waldren survived shooting herself and there are reports of a third suicide, all for love of Harry in the early 1900s.

In 1911, he changed his surname to Allen after being targeted by the reformers and police in Seattle, who repeatedly arrested him. In the same year, he was arrested for selling alcohol to Native Americans. He was arrested again the following year in Portland, Oregon, with Isabelle Maxwell and charged with taking her there for immoral purposes, as she had a record of prostitution. Instead, he was imprisoned (as a woman) for vagrancy. Whilst serving his 90 days, he became part of a study by an anthropologist and social reformer, Miriam Van Waters, who was sympathetic, but failed to accept Harry's choice of gender.

By 1917, Harry (ex-bartender and convicted criminal) was working with the police in Washington state, who had introduced prohibition. Then, in 1919, his father, who was a violent drunkard, stabbed him in the back after a quarrel, but he survived. He moved on from alcohol to opium, but that led to another arrest in 1920. He contracted syphilis and died in 1922 from syphilitic meningitis.

Hatshepsut
(circa 1508–1458 BCE)

Hatshepsut was a Bronze Age, 18th Dynasty Egyptian pharaoh. Hatshepsut was the most notable of the female pharaohs and the only one to become king. The others include Neithhotep (b. circa 3100 BCE) who may have been the earliest and who was grandmother to Merneith (circa 3000 BCE), who was queen and regent. She was also named as pharoah in the tomb of her successor, her son Den. Sobekneferu ruled for four years from 1806 BCE and was the last pharoah of the 12th Dynasty. Other women ruled, such as Nitocris aka Nitiqret (2184–2181 BCE), Nefertiti (1370–1330 BCE) and Cleopatra VII (circa 51–12 BCE).

Hatshepsut was the daughter of Thutmose I and whilst a child was designated 'God's Wife to Amun'. This enabled her to gain wealth, property and knowledge. She was destined to become the King's Great Wife, but two brothers and her father died when she was 16 and then so did Thutmose II. An illegitimate half-brother was selected to become king with Hatshepsut ruling as regent. She gained religious, military and political support in order to hold on to power, and she performed a king's duties. These acts were detailed in inscriptions and portrayed on carvings with her wearing female costume but a king's headdress.

In 1478 BCE she crowned herself king, probably by the seventh year of her reign, rather than queen of Egypt. She ensured that in all future carvings she was represented in full male regalia, including the false beard of the pharaohs.

She sent trading expeditions far afield, including to the Land of Punt (probably around current day Somalia, Djibouti and Eritrea). Myrrh trees were brought back and, for the first time, replanted. Hatshepsut used charred frankincense as kohl eyeliner also for the first time. She also led military campaigns in Nubia, Kush and current-day Palestine and Syria. All her efforts were successful and consolidated her power. Of the ten mega structures she had built, the greatest was the temple at Deir el-Bahari near the Valley of the Kings. It was called Djeser-Djeseru and contained magnificent carvings honouring her. She was honoured after her death and succeeded by Thutmose III, whom she had trained. However, when his son was due to succeed him, he appears to have attempted to portray a smooth succession of Thutmose kings by disfiguring inscriptions and carvings of Hatshepsut. Current restoration work is placing her back in her legitimate place.

Herculine Adélaïde Barbin *aka* Alexina *and also* Abel Barbin (1838–1868)

Herculine was a 19th century intersex person who always self-identified as female. They were brought up as a girl by a poor mother before being given a charity scholarship for schooling in a convent. Thereafter, they lived in a training college and then in a Catholic boarding school they were sent to. Philosopher and historian Michel Foucault republished the memoir that Herculine wrote in Paris, in which they call themselves Alexina, including others' contemporary reports and articles that had been published. He drew attention to their life spent in the different institutions and only with females (a sole parent, clergy, teachers, students, friends and female lovers).

By Herculine's own account, they enjoyed the 'calme delicieux' of their cloistered life and relationships with fellow teachers and students. They were effectively a woman having lesbian affairs. They had a slim build and a developing beard. Neither the physical appearance, its changes (which included some abdominal pains), or the different affairs drew attention to Herculine. They had developed a serious love affair with a fellow teaching student called Sara, which continued when they were both sent to the same school. This and their developing body caused Herculine to seek advice from a priest.

The priest referred Herculine to doctors, who humiliated them with a very aggressive and intrusive examination. There were reports of a 'mélange' of sexual characteristics, defined later as male pseudo-hermaphrodism. However, the doctors at the time concluded that they were more male than female. Foucault theorized that they may have thought it was preferable that they were a man having an affair with Sara, rather than a lesbian woman. Subsequently, Herculine was forced to leave the school and their friends to live and seek work as a man in Paris. They only found a few low-paid jobs and did not settle into this new, unwanted life. Herculine became destitute and depressed at the contrast with their earlier life. After a few years they died by gassing themselves. Herculine's birthday was the 8th November, which is now designated as the Intersex Day of Remembrance. Virginia Woolf, Jeffrey Eugenides, Kate Bornstein, Judith Butler and others have written works that were inspired by or were about Herculine.

Hermaphroditus

In 8 CE, the Greek poet Ovid wrote about Hermaphroditus and the water nymph Salmacis. In his *Metamorphoses*, she saw him bathing in a pool (in some versions it was a well) and fell so in love that she would not be separated from him. The gods answered her prayers and joined them together permanently so that they became a female figure with male genitals. Using 'they' as the pronoun for non-binary people is therefore very appropriate.

The *Metamorphoses* features other similar characters, including Tiresias, Iphis and Caens (aka Caeneus). Aristophanes' version of hermaphrodites retains the individual selves joined together, rather than combining fully in Ovid's portrayal. Ovid did also question the possible futures of his creation and what their experiences would be, basing these in part on the realities of intersex peoples' lives. Hermaphroditus was also the child of Hermes and Aphrodite, and the name combines both of theirs and represents fertilization, productivity and marriage (which binds male and female together). Hermes and Aphrodite were both deities of sexuality, and Aphrodite could also appear as male and female to mortals. Some early cults worshipped Aphroditus who, for the Romans, was Venus Barbata (included in this book). They are also known by the other names of Atlantius and Atlantiades (who is represented in the modern Wonder Woman stories). Representation of Hermaphroditus have been popular in Classic and mythological art throughout history, as in the Roman statue illustrated here.

There are many parallel versions of Hermaphroditus, in Greek religion Zeus and Gaia also created another double-gendered god called Agdistis. The Hindu deity Shiva, like Aristophanes' hermaphrodites, joins together with his consort Parvati and is transformed into Ardhanarishvara (with a male right half and a female left). Also Hinduism, the androgynous Purusha's two-sex halves copulate and create all life.

Jacqueline-Charlotte Dufresnoy *aka* Coccinelle (1931–2006)

Coccinelle was born in Paris and from the age of four began to question her gender. She dyed her hair a platinum blonde and took to wearing women's clothing after being conscripted and then discharged within a week from the army. A red dress with black polka dots was a favourite and reminded people of a ladybird ('coccinelle' in French). In 1953, she began appearing in the Parisian drag cabaret at Chez Madame Arthur's and then at the 'sister' club, the Carrousel. She was the first of the troupe, which included April Ashley, Amanda Lear and Bambi, to begin taking hormones and, in 1958, also the first to have gender reassignment surgery. They all went to Dr Georges Burou's Casablanca clinic after the success of Coccinelle's surgery. She got a new birth certificate that read 'Jacqueline-Charlotte born woman'. The following year she appeared in a racy documentary *Europe by Night*, the first of six films she appeared in. In 1960, she married François Bonnet, a journalist.

Coincidently, it was April Ashley's divorce in 1970 that stopped trans people being able to marry in the UK for decades, nor would they be able to change birth certificates for about as long. However, Jacqueline-Charlotte had been baptised in her new name before her marriage, and then, to get a divorce from François she had to declare that she was still a man. It meant she got her divorce and married twice more. But this resulted in her excommunication, and the French state stopped changing trans peoples' documents for years until till 1974. She published *Coccinelle by Coccinelle* in 1987 and continued performing, including at Romy Haag's club in Berlin, until 1990. She was a trans activist and founded the organization 'Devenir Femme' ('Becoming a Woman' in French) and a centre that researched gender identities and dysphoria. She owned a traditional cabaret in Marseilles until she had the stroke that killed her.

Coccinelle
Star du Carrousel de Paris

Chercher
la femme

James Allen

(1788–1830)

After a fatal accident, James was taken to St Thomas' Hospital in London where doctors discovered that he was female. At the time, he was employed as a sawyer at a ship-wright in St Saviour's Dock in Bermondsey. He had suffered a crushed skull when a large piece of timber fell on him. James had worked for a few years as a groom, as a publican and as a labourer before working at different ship-wrights. Most of his work was quite physical. At the inquest into his death, fellow workers also expressed their surprise that James was anatomically female. Abigail Allen, also called Mary, his wife of 21 years, swore in an affidavit that she knew nothing of his true sex. She had met James when they had both been in service to the same gentleman and had married at St Giles' Church in Camberwell in December 1808. He had been an industrious husband, but was sometimes rough with her, according to Mary. One report stated that they had argued and he had hit her on the morning of his death. She said that he wrapped his chest in linen and wore thick waistcoats, which he justified by a need to protect himself during his work outside.

At the inquest, Mary said that she thought that James was originally from Lowestoft. There were doubts about her assertion that she was ignorant of James' sex, especially as she had nursed him during the times that he was very ill. As well as supporting her for so long, it was thought that he had some savings. It is even claimed that James had visited a brother in the East Indies and returned with over a thousand pounds, which he banked and never used. He also had a box of papers and valuables, which he kept by the bed, and he always carried documents and money in a linen wallet. Mary probably claimed all these. She remained at their lodging in East Lane, near where James worked, but reverted to her maiden name, Naylor. She was subject to so much harassment that she needed police protection. Some of this was caused by rumours that she was a cross-dressing man. James, despite the length of their marriage, was termed her 'pretended husband'.

There were theories that James was intersex, but the post-mortem revealed that James had given birth and a son was reported to have been found. The story of this 'female husband' was celebrated in a pamphlet and a ballad and was reported widely in newspapers.

James Grey *aka* Hannah Snell
(1723–1792)

By the 18th century, more women, disguised as men, served in the military than previously, such as Christian Davis, Phoebe Hessel and others. Some cross-dressed for socio-economic reasons, or to escape the sexual discrimination and constraints of that period. A distinctive few stayed in that new identity after it was still necessary, or safe. Other examples of female soldiers and sailors are included here, such as James Barry, Samuel Bundy, Albert Cashier, Francisco de Loyola, Laurence Michael Dillon, James Grey, Mark Read and John Taylor. And also a hundred women, including Maria van Antwerpen, are estimated to have done this in Holland during the 1700s.

An impoverished and pregnant Hannah Snell was deserted by her husband. After the child died, she joined the army in Coventry in 1745 using her brother-in-law's name. She later gave the reason that she wanted to find her husband. As James, he managed to avoid discovery, despite the problems that urination, menstruation, etc. may have caused. He did also escape detection and manage to survive when, in 1746, he had to take 500 lashes 'on the bare' and fled from the army.

James travelled to Portsmouth and joined the Royal Marines. The regiment sailed to India via Lisbon in HMS *Swallow*.

He faced storms and diseases, as well as a lady who almost married him. He received 12 shots in the legs and groin and lost a finger during a battle at Pondicherry in 1748. Rather than risking being discovered, James dug a musket ball out of his groin himself and survived again. He recovered and joined a ship to return to England and resumed his life as a woman.

Hannah did get the pay due to her for the four and a half years of legitimate service and was, for a time, a celebrity, unlike the male cross-dressers at the time, who were prosecuted. She did first reveal her gender to fellow Marines in 1750 in a pub and then, on their advice, successfully petitioned the Duke of Cumberland for her pension of £30 a month. She used her celebrity to appear in uniform in theatres as a singer and performing military routines. She then ran a pub in Wapping, also wearing a uniform, and published her autobiography. She married Richard Elyse, a carpenter, in 1759 and had sons with him. She later married Richard Habgood in 1772. In 1791, she was sent to the Bethlehem Royal Hospital (Bedlam) and died of syphilis a year later. She was buried in the graveyard of the Royal Hospital Chelsea, alongside her fellow soldiers, as she requested.

John Taylor *aka* Mary Anne Talbot (1778–1808)

John's life was well known through the embellished autobiography *The Life and Surprising Adventures of Mary Anne Talbot in the Name of John Taylor* and a broadside ballad 'The Female Drummer'. Mary Anne was one of 16 children that Lord Talbot had with his mistress, and she was sent to an aged guardian, Richard Sucker, when she was fourteen. He stole her inheritance and passed her over to a Captain Essex Bowen, who made her his mistress. He disguised her as his servant, John Taylor, on a voyage with his regiment, which was diverted to join the Duke of York's troops in France. Bowen volunteered John as a drummer boy. They joined in the siege of Valenciennes, where John was wounded in the chest by a musket ball and on the neck by a sword and where Bowen was killed. John deserted and joined French Captain Le Sage's ship, which was captured by British ships. John became a cabin boy on one.

They fought two French ships in June 1794, and John's leg was almost severed by grapeshot. After some treatment in Gosport, John continued on as a sailor and signed on to the uss *Vesuvius*. John and others were imprisoned in Dunkirk after it was defeated by French ships. In 1796, John was released and sailed to New York, with Captain John Field on board the *Ariel* as a mate, or possibly a clerk. Field invited John to his home where his niece wanted him as her husband, but John sailed back on the *Ariel* to London. There, John may have entered into a long-term relationship with a woman.

John's adventures were first written about in the *Times* of November 4th 1799 whilst again having the leg wound treated. They were also repeated in John Ashton's *Old Times, Kirby's Wonderful and Eccentric Museum and Magazine of Remarkable Characters* (also see Dr John Theodora de Verdion) and the 1804 Naval Chronicles and are currently in the *Oxford Dictionary of National Biography*. Prints of Mary Anne are held by the National Maritime Museum. Mary Anne tried to get a pension, worked on the stage and sometimes relied on charity, but eventually fell into debt and was imprisoned in Newgate prison. On her release, she worked as a servant for Kirby, her publisher, but died three years later.

Karl M. Baer
(1885–1956)

Karl was identified as a girl and named Martha when he was born in Germany, though there were doubts about the baby's gender due to hypospadias, a displacement of the urethra that caused confusion about his genitals. Karl's semi-autobiographical *Memoirs of a Man's Maiden Years* is still currently available, having been published in 1907 under the pseudonym N. O. Body. The book was very popular, and film versions were made in 1912 and 1919. In it he wrote that he was a boy who was raised as a girl. Naturally, he had trouble fitting in to the expectations demanded of him.

He was brought up in Arolsen in central Germany but moved to Hamburg in 1904. There he was a suffragette and worked as a social worker. He also participated in the lesbian life there and became an activist in the Zionist B'nai Brith. He started presenting as a man in 1904. By then he had male characteristics such as a deep voice, masculine features and facial hair. He also adopted stereotypical male behaviour and started smoking cigars and drinking beer. He began a love affair with Beile Halpern, a married woman. However, his intersex characteristics were identified by doctors treating him after a tram accident and also because he was presenting as a man but had the documents of a female. He then went to Dr Magnus Hirschfeld at his Institute for Sexual Research in Berlin. Hirschfeld had written the afterword to Karl's book. Karl was diagnosed as a male pseudo-hermaphrodite and was provided with the first sex reassignment, or corrective, surgery in 1906.

In January 1907, Karl was allowed to change sex legally and get his male birth certificate so that he could marry Beile, who had divorced. She died in 1909 and Karl was married again, to Elza Max. He also headed a branch of B'nai Brith. In 1937 he was arrested by the Gestapo and tortured. In a way this saved his life, because, on his release, he fled to Palestine and also escaped the fate of many other Jews, as well as Hirschfeld's clinic, staff and patients, like Dora Richter. He became an insurance agent and lived in a polyamorous relationship with his wife and his secretary, Gitla Fish. Interestingly, the 'M' initial in his name stood for Martha at first. Later, Karl said it was for Max, but Meir ended up on his headstone in the Kiryat Shaul Cemetery in Tel Aviv.

Laurence Michael Dillon

(1915–1962)

Dillon studied at St Anne's College, Oxford. Dillon was president of the ladies rowing club and took his Blue (the highest sporting achievement at Oxford) in 1938. Dillon worked at a research laboratory after graduating and in 1939 consulted Dr George Foss. Dr Foss used testosterone as treatment for Dillon, who was also referred to a psychiatrist. He made his patient's condition public and forced Dillon, by then passing as male, to flee. Whilst being treated in hospital for hypoglycaemia, he met a plastic surgeon who performed a double mastectomy on him and provided evidence for the change of birth certificate in 1944.

In 1945, Dillon became a medical student at Trinity College Dublin. This time he was on the men's rowing team. He had 13 gender reassignment operations from Dr Harold Gillies, including a phalloplasty, during the holidays from university until 1949. It is believed that Dillon was the world's first female to male (FTM) transsexual to undergo phalloplasty. Dr Gillies had reconstructed penises for injured soldiers, and he had to give a false diagnosis, of acute hypospadias, to hide the true nature of the surgeries. In 1946, Dillon published a book about transsexuality, *Self: A Study in Endocrinology and Ethics*. This drew Roberta Cowell's attention to him. He fell in love with her and then helped her achieve her transition by performing a (then illegal) orchiectomy. Roberta's gender reassignment surgery was also completed by Dr Gillies in 1951.

Dillon was outed by the *Daily Express* in 1958 whilst serving as a ship's doctor. He was a member of the aristocracy and was listed as Laurence Michael in Debrett's Peerage. Confirmation of his changed gender was given to the reporters by his brother, Robert. After the outing he had to flee again, this time to India. He became a Buddhist monk, changing his name, again, to Lobzang Jivaha, or Jivaka, and wrote books on the religion. He died aged only 47, possibly due to the poor conditions and very limited diet he had to endure.

Lili Elbe *aka* Lili Ilse Elvenes (1882–1931)

Lili is now famous because of the biographical film about her, *Danish Girl*, starring Eddie Redmayne. It details much of the chronology of her transition and operations. She changed her name to Lili Ilse Elvenes in 1930. The name Lili Elbe was a pseudonym given to her in sensationalist newspaper articles.

Lili and her wife, Gerda, settled in Paris in 1912. She started to present as Lili in public, pretending to be Gerda's sister, and she also posed for her paintings. These works by Gerda, who presented herself as a lesbian, became quite fashionable.

In 1930, Lili had the first of a series of four gender reassignment surgeries. This was an orchiectomy that was carried out in Berlin by Dr Ludwig Levy-Lenz, who was supervised by Dr Magnus Hirschfeld. The subsequent operations were done at the Dresden Municipal Women's Clinic by Dr Kurt Warnekros, a Nazi party member. He followed the vaginoplasty techniques of Dr Erwin Gohrbandt, who pioneered the surgery on Dora Richter a short time before. Dr Gohrbandt was later a decorated Luftwaffe surgeon. In the second operation, an ovary was implanted. The third operation was to remove the penis and the scrotum. Dr Warnekros attempted to create a vagina and transplant a uterus. The latter was rejected, and the remedial surgeries caused the infection and heart attack that killed Lili.

Hirschfeld's Berlin Institute archive was destroyed by Nazis in 1933 and Allied bombing destroyed those in Dresden in 1945, leaving the history of German research and original work on Lili, Dora and others very incomplete. In July 2019 a new digital archive was launched at www.lilielbe.org on the 100th anniversary of the founding of Hirschfeld's Institute. As well as restoring records of the original institute and collecting those about Lili, it aims to create a resource for research into transgender history.

Mademoiselle Lefort
(circa 1800–1868)

Lefort's portrait is based on a contemporary engraving in *The London Medical Repository and Review*, Volume 9, 1818, though it does look like it may not be too authentic a likeness. The article in that journal refers to them as a Parisian hermaphrodite and says that they were exhibited in Spring Gardens that year as a 'bearded lady', aged about nineteen. Spring Gardens was the original name for the Vauxhall Pleasure Gardens near Kennington, which provided entertainments from the thousands of participants and was illuminated by glass lamps hung in the trees. The Royal Surrey Zoological Gardens, another pleasure garden, was also situated nearby.

Lefort's appearance was described in intimate detail in the article. They were reported to be five feet tall with a beard and moustache. Their more female form was described as 'exceedingly beautiful' and 'voluptuous'. They had full breasts, small hands and feet and a feminine voice. It also reported the results of what must have been a medical examination by a doctor into the anatomical and physiological characteristics of one they labelled a 'phenomenon'. The report, which also indicated that they were an exceptional true hermaphrodite, reveals that the writer, at least, had not encountered anyone similar before. An infant-sized small penis was also described, rather than a possible clitoris, with a partial labia and no testes. No urethral opening was seen and, strangely, there were a number of small openings that emitted urine. They also reported that there was another small canal a little lower. More urine and menstrual blood both came from this orifice, which led the doctor to presume that a separate urethra and bladder joined together inside the canal. The article even described a strong male sexual desire for females and reported that this desire had been regularly satisfied.

There is a surviving handbill for another exhibition of Lefort, this one in an apartment at 25 Queen Street, Golden Square, with an admittance price of 2s 6d. It must predate the show above, as this handbill is headed, 'FACTS! AMAZING FACTS! Never Exhibited in England, Mademoiselle LEFORT, IN HER NINETEENTH YEAR, A first rate Phaenomenon, OF FRENCH PRODUCTION.' It continues to describe Lefort in great detail.

Marguerite Malaure
(b. 1665)

Marguerite faced the prejudice and curiosity of the church hierarchy, the authorities and the 17th century French population of the Ancien Régime because of her (perceived) hermaphrodism and gender confusion. She lived two centuries before the famous intersex person Herculine Barbin. They shared similar problems, and both also created anxieties and difficulties for the establishment.

Like many other intersex pioneers, most of the information about Marguerite has been preserved from court records. Marguerite was born near Toulouse and was baptized as female. After being orphaned early, she was brought up by a priest. At 21, she fell ill and was admitted to the Hôtel-Dieu Saint-Jacques hospital in Toulouse. She had a very female appearance and did menstruate, but several doctors and the vicars general decreed that she was a hermaphrodite (which she never accepted). They also decided that she was predominately male and therefore had to dress as such. Because people were so insistent that they see her undressed, she fled from Toulouse. She arrived in Bordeaux in female clothing again and resumed working as a lady's maid. Unfortunately, she was recognized five years later and, being criminalized, was put on trial. The magistrates decided that on the threat of being whipped, she had to accept the male name of Arnaud de Malaure and continue her life as a man. Since she could no longer work as a lady's maid, Marguerite had to rely on charity to survive.

Marguerite showed some spirit and initiative after this. She travelled to consult the Parisian doctor Helvétius. He decided that she was female and that some of the confusion was because she had a uterine prolapse and some of her uterus was protruding from her vagina. One of the likeliest causes of that condition in her case was that she had suffered some trauma during an undisclosed childbirth. She was referred for surgery to correct the prolapse in the care of a surgeon, Barthélmy Saviard. He completed the operation whilst putting her on exhibition to earn some money. But the doctors had no power to change the previous decision of the court, and Marguerite was still left with no means of earning money. She took her case to the king, Louis XIV. By 1691, a commission into her case was established and rescinded the previous court's decision so that Marguerite was able to complete her life as a woman.

Mark Read *aka* Mary Read

(1685 or 1690–1721)

Read's mother was getting maintenance for a son from her in-laws when her husband died. She dressed Mary as the son when he also died to continue getting the support. Mary continued as Mark Read to become a footman at the age of 13. Mark then became a British soldier and then a Flemish soldier and gained a reputation for bravery. She married another soldier, and they ran an inn until he died prematurely. Mary became Mark again and returned to the military. She sailed to the West Indies and when the ship was attacked by pirates, she joined their crew. Mark became a privateer before joining John 'Calico Jack' Rackham's pirate crew, still as Mark Read. Anne Bonny (12 years younger) was Calico Jack's lover, and she used male disguise during the fighting. They seized ships and recruited crews in the Caribbean during the Golden Age of Piracy.

Mary fell in love with one of the sailors and eventually they became lovers. Mary defended her lover by fighting and winning a duel with a pirate who was feuding with him. In 1720, their ship was captured by the Jamaican authorities, and all were arrested. Those on the ship were sentenced to be hung, but Anne's and Mary's pregnancies saved them. Unfortunately, Mary caught a fever in the prison and died. Details of Anne's future are vague, but most sources give a possible date of her death as 1782. Anne and Mary were among the most famous pirates at the time (and also possibly since then).

John Gay's 1728 opera *Polly* celebrates a female pirate. Grace O'Malley (1530–1600) was the daughter of a chieftain and clan leader and called a pirate by her enemies, the forces of Elizabeth I (whom she met). The first female pirate may have been Teuta of Illyria (in the area from Croatia to Albania). She became queen in 231 BCE and attacked the ships of neighbouring countries to keep them at bay. Madame Cheng (Ching Shih) operated hundreds of ships crewed by tens of thousands of men and women. She died at the age of 69 in 1844. None of the others adopted a cross-gendered identity like Mary/Mark, not even Anne Bonny.

Marsha P. Johnson
(1945–1992)

Marsha came out upon moving to New York City in 1963. She gave herself a new name and persona and survived by taking part in drag shows and by street prostitution. Marsha's style varied from the masculine to the feminine and any variety in between. Marsha went to the Stonewall gay bar in Greenwich Village as soon as it allowed women and drag queens in. There were frequent raids on the Stonewall Inn, with robberies, beatings and arrests by the police. In the early hours of June 28th, 1969, Johnson is cited as igniting the Stonewall Riots by throwing either a glass at a mirror or a brick at the police (bricks were weapons she had been known to use – breaking a police car window with one during the riots and another time swinging her bag loaded with a pair of bricks at police trying to arrest her on the streets). She is also reported to have shouted, 'I got my civil rights'.

In 1970, she set up STAR (Street Transvestite Action Revolutionaries) with Sylvia Rivera. This radical LGBTQI+ collective provided housing and support to homeless queer youth and sex workers. Johnson was also an AIDS activist with AIDS Coalition to Unleash Power (ACT UP). From 1972 until 1990, Marsha also performed with a number of groups like The Cockettes, the Angels of Light and the Hot Peaches. She was also one of Andy Warhol's Factory personnel.

After the 1992 New York Pride March, Marsha P. Johnson's body was found in the Hudson River and, despite visible wounds and reports of her being harassed, her death was judged to be suicide.

You can find out more about Marsha through the feature films, documentaries and online content about her, including *Pay It No Mind: The Life and Times of Marsha P. Johnson*. The documentary gives a good idea of how loved she was and what an amazing personality she had. The Johnson Park has been delayed due to criticism of the lack of community involvement, but formally the East River State Park was renamed the Marsha P. Johnson State Park in 2020. In August 2021, a bust of her was unveiled in Christopher Park near the Stonewall Inn.

Mary Frith *aka* Moll Cutpurse
(circa 1584–1659)

Mary had been troublesome even in childhood. Her family attempted to ship young Mary off to America, but she jumped ship and joined a gang of pickpockets (nicknamed cutpurses for their method of getting purses). She was repeatedly caught and sometimes punished by being burnt on the hand. She continually presented herself in male breeches and a doublet, whilst behaving badly: drinking, smoking and swearing. She wasn't alone; Islington innkeeper Long Meg and others had established the cross-dressing woman as a fairly common sight, and feminine men were common too.

At least a part of Mary/Moll's income came from performing – telling stories and singing bawdy songs – whilst also playing the lute. She did this all while wearing men's clothes. One suggestion is that she performed in order to distract customers while her gang robbed them. Despite some further punishments, she gained considerable popularity, or notoriety. This made her the subject of two plays: John Day's 1610 drama *The Madde Pranckes of Mery Mall of the Bankside* and Thomas Dekker and Thomas Middleton's 1611 *The Roaring Girl*. Moll was arrested because of her 'immodest and lascivious' afterpiece during the play. She was imprisoned then, and later in the year she was arrested again. This time she had to voice her confession from St Paul's churchyard but was reportedly 'maudlin drunck' while she did it. Many other accounts and interpretations of her life have been written ever since her death.

She accepted a £20 wager from William Banks, which challenged her to ride from Charing Cross to Shoreditch dressed as a man as usual. She won the bet, but did so carrying a banner, blowing a trumpet and riding a performing horse called Marocco. By 1614 she had achieved some wealth, owning a house with servants, and she bred mastiffs. She also obtained a husband in a marriage of convenience in 1614 (to a Lewknor Markham), which shielded her from some prosecutions. It's certain that she was dealing in stolen goods and continuing to work as a 'fence'. Less certain is that she used her house as a brothel and as a place for wealthy women to meet male prostitutes. She has been called a transsexual, transvestite, lesbian and asexual, but may be best described as an early genderqueer person.

Miss Fanny Winifred Park *aka* Frederick William Park (1846–1881)

Right

Lady Stella Clinton *aka* Thomas Ernest Boulton (1847–1904)

Left

Miss Fanny Winifred Park and Lady Stella Clinton were both arrested in 1870 at the Strand Theatre, which they were attending dressed in women's clothes (pictured). They had taken a private box and used the ladies' lavatory. The police had been observing them for some time and had gathered details of their lifestyles and acquaintances. They performed, as well as keeping and going about in their women's clothes in a house in Wakefield Street, Bloomsbury, which now has a blue plaque. Though 'personating a woman' in public was a misdemeanour, they and others were charged with the felony of sodomy instead. The following morning, after a night in the cells, they appeared in female dress before the Bow Street Magistrates' Court, after being refused permission to change.

Stella/Boulton stated that she was Lord Arthur Clinton's wife and that they had lived together. Clinton, a Liberal MP for Newark, did not appear, as he died soon after the trial had started. Some have proposed that he faked his death, or died by suicide, despite scarlet fever being the official cause of death. However, despite year-long police surveillance, very intimate medical examinations and the display of photographs and love letters, there was no proof of sodomy and they were acquitted and able to resume their stage careers.

Neil McKenna's 2013 book, *Fanny and Stella*, gives a very full and accurate picture of them and the London they inhabited. They were even at one time bound over to keep the peace after being mistaken for women whilst actually being dressed as the men they were.

In August 2020, during a break in the Covid-19 lockdowns, the Garden Theatre at the Eagle pub in Kennington, London, staged their camp musical based (surprisingly accurately) on Fanny and Stella's story. It was very well received by the socially distanced and mask-wearing audiences, who were able to appreciate songs like 'Has Anyone Seen My Fanny'.

Roberta (Betty) Cowell
(1918–2011)

Betty Cowell studied engineering at University College London and met her future wife, Diana Carpenter, there. Diana became the first British woman to get an engineering degree, and both Diana and Roberta also raced cars. Roberta joined the RAF as a pupil pilot in 1935 and married Diana before being posted to France. A daughter, Anne, was born in 1942 and a second daughter, Diana, in 1944. During a last tour of duty, Roberta's Spitfire crashed, and she ended up in Stalag Luft I, which had terrible conditions. After the war, Roberta suffered from depression, and, after using drugs and alcohol, underwent psychotherapy. She separated from Diana in 1948.

Around this time, she cross-dressed consistently and, after reading Laurence Michael Dillon's book, *Self: A Study in Endocrinology and Ethics*, corresponded with him. When they began meeting, Michael fell in love with Roberta. He wanted to propose, but a marriage would only be possible if Roberta could change sex. At the time castration was illegal, but Michael, who was a medical student, managed to perform a successful orchiectomy on her. With that, Roberta got an intersex diagnosis. Then, in May, 1951, Dr Harold Gillies performed the first gender reassignment surgery in the UK on her. Later that month, Roberta was able to become legally female.

In July of 1951, Michael passed his final examinations, but Roberta turned down his proposal. Instead, Betty, as she liked to be called, began her 30-year partnership with Lisa Morrell, who had supported her throughout the treatments. She disowned her daughters after her 1952 divorce from Diana and refused contact with them. Roberta resumed racing and attempted to start various businesses. The expensive lifestyle she had with Lisa and need for costly hormones eventually bankrupted her. She did write articles about her transition for the *Picture Post* magazine for £8000. The accuracy of Roberta's articles is said to be debatable and there is some homophobic and even transphobic content. Lisa died in 2009 and Betty died in 2011.

Rosaria (Rosa) Mifsud

(late 18th century)

Rosa was born at Luqa in Malta. They went before the Grand Court of the Order of St John's Castellania and the Spanish Grandmaster, Francisco Ximenes, in 1774 at the age of 17 to petition for a change of gender designation to male. The court appointed officials to interview Rosa's family and neighbours and were told that Rosa had been seen urinating against a wall like a man. They appointed the physician-in-chief and a senior surgeon from the Order's Holy Infirmary to examine Rosa, who had been brought up as female. The doctors found 'the male is the dominant one',[5] but Rosa had some secondary sex characteristics more typical of the other gender. The very detailed reports described a small penis with a urethral opening at its base and folds at either side, like labia, containing the testes. The doctors found a rudimentary vagina, which was too narrow for them to insert a little finger. Rosa did not have a female's mammary development but did have a deep voice. The consequence was that the grandmaster took the final decision that Rosa should only wear male clothing thereafter. Rosa was intersex, but, in the language of the time, was defined as a pseudo-hermaphrodite, because they hadn't got both an ovary and testes that a true hermaphrodite would have.

In 2013, the Marta Kwitt theatre group, founded by Immanuel Mifsud, performed the play 'The Strange Case of Rosario Mifsud' at the National Archives of Malta, housed in the Grandmaster's Palace in Rabat. They also presented it at the National Library in Valetta in 2014.

Malta has been at the forefront of LGBTQI+ rights since the 20th century. Same-sex sexual activity with an equal age of consent was made legal in 1973. Employment discrimination was made illegal in 2004, and many other anti-discrimination laws were introduced in 2014 and 2017. In 2015, the Gender Identity, Gender Expression and Sex Characteristics Act became law in Malta. It provided intersex people with some of the most progressive protections and outlawed non-consensual cosmetic medical treatments to alter sex anatomy. It was the first country to do this. The act also includes protections from discrimination and provides a simplified method of changing legal gender, as well as allowing for a non-binary identity.

---

5   Savona-Ventura, C. (2015) *Knight Hospitaller Medicine in Malta [1530–1798]*. Lulu: Charles Savona-Ventura, p.114.

Samuel Bundy *aka* Sarah Paul
(b. 1739)

Based on court records and reports in contemporary newspapers, Sarah became Samuel when they were 13 or 14 years of age during an affair with an artist. The artist disguised them as a boy and pretended that he was the father for the year they lived together, perhaps to avoid Samuel's mother. Still as a boy, he then became a sailor and went to sea for a year. On returning to London, Samuel became a painter's male assistant. During his employment, Samuel began a love affair with Mary Parlour, who lived at the King's Head public house in Southwark. They married in October 1759, but Samuel claimed that he was ill and couldn't have sex for a while. Samuel lost his job and Mary supported him, and she later didn't support the prosecution of Samuel for defrauding her. In his search for work, Samuel returned to sea, first on a warship, the *Prince Frederick*, and then on a merchant ship. There did seem to be love between the couple as Samuel returned to Mary, and after his arrest Mary stood by him so that Samuel had to be released. When Samuel was confronted by a suspicious landlord before he was reported and sent for trial, he had defended his lack of a penis with the statement, 'I owe this to a shark in the West Indies'.

He wasn't prosecuted for becoming Mary's husband but for what was classed as a financial fraud against her. Their landlord might have spread word about Samuel's identity. He became a celebrity during the arrest and trial, with many women wanting to marry him and others giving him money. After the dismissal, the judge did order that his male clothes should be burnt and the marriage was annulled. It seems that ended Samuel/Sarah's non-binary/trans life. At the end of 1760, Sarah (as a woman) married again, this time to William Kitchen. No further details are available. Other similar 18th-century examples include Ann Marrow, who was pilloried for cross-dressing as well as marrying three women. She was attacked by people so violently that they blinded her. Two others in this book are Charles Hamilton (who was flogged) and James Allen, whose female gender wasn't revealed until his death. Another, James How, was involved in a case against his blackmailer, but wasn't prosecuted himself.

Sporus
(49–69 CE)

In the ancient world, there were fewer prohibitions on switching gender and varying sexuality than the modern world imposes. Interestingly, there are parallels between the Sporus/Nero story and Polly Katt/Howard Hughes story: they both arranged the castration of their cross-dressing mistresses. The early cultures of the Roman, Egyptian and Greek worlds provide multiple other similar examples, both real and legendary.

Emperor Nero (37–68 CE) ruled from 54 CE until his death. He had a number of marriages, firstly to Claudia Octavia, whose mother married Claudius and, reputedly, persuaded him to nominate Nero as his successor. Poppaea Sabina was Nero's next wife, and he was her third marriage (her second was to Otho, who very briefly succeeded Nero as emperor). In 65 CE, Nero killed Poppaea Sabina by kicking her whilst she was pregnant (or she may have just died from complications during her pregnancy). Nero then had a brief marriage to a freedman called Pythagoras (with Nero as the bride). Nero also married Statilia Messalina.

Following that, Nero was attracted to the young Sporus, who closely resembled Poppaea. He had him castrated (so the illustration, which is based on a statue of Poppaea, is also a likeness of Sporus). It was a procedure that masters of puer delicatus, or 'boy toys', inflicted to preserve their youthful looks. Nero went further and married Sporus, presented her as female, called her Poppaea and made her empress. The Praetorian Guard abandoned their support for Nero, and the Senate declared him an enemy of the people. When Nero committed suicide, rather than face the expected execution, he had Sporus with him.

Sporus continued to be called Poppaea by his next partner, a Praetorian prefect called Nymphidius Sabinus, who was killed shortly after. Finally, Sporus was with Otho, who only lasted three months as emperor before being killed by Vitellius. Sporus was going to be raped and killed at a gladiator show but committed suicide in order to avoid that fate.

Emperor Domitian had a virtual marriage to the freedman eunuch Earinus, Alexander the Great had a Persian eunuch lover called Bagoas and the Egyptian Ptolemy VIII had Pothinus (see also Elagabalus in this book). Male to male marriages were not uncommon but became rarer as the empire was Christianized and prohibitions were introduced. Sappho and the writer Lucian, amongst others, refer to lesbian sex and Lucian also refers to Sappho's home island of Lesbos.

Sylvia Rivera
(1951–2002)

Rivera had Puerto Rican and Venezuelan parents, but she was an orphan at the age of three and was living on the streets in New York (in the 42nd Street area frequented by drag queens) at eleven and became a child prostitute. She was helped by local drag queens, especially Marsha P. Johnson. She was homeless and a drug addict for long periods of her life. In the 1960s, because of her own experiences, she involved herself in the civil rights and anti–Vietnam War movements, feminist groups and prisoner aid and black organizations like the Black Panthers. Her activism was particularly directed at helping people like herself, who suffered the worst discrimination.

She was one of the leaders of the 1969 Stonewall Riots and a founding member of Street Transvestite Action Revolutionaries (STAR), which helped the homeless young and trans women of colour. She also opposed gays' discrimination against transgender people, drag queens and lesbians. Watch the online footage of the 1973 Pride Rally. She had to fight not to be put at the back of the march and was refused the opportunity to speak from the platform. When she did, she was booed and yelled at, but by the end of her 'Y'all Better Quiet Down' speech she was cheered.

It is extraordinary, considering her status now and all the work she did for her community that she still continued to be poor and homeless. She continued the fight for the equality legislations that were being introduced. Unfortunately, Rivera had to fight some of the LGBTQI+ organizations and leaders who still wanted to exclude transgender and drag culture from the deals they were making. She travelled to Italy for the Millennium March in 2000 and was honoured with the title of the 'Mother of All Gay People'. She always refused to accept Marsha P. Johnson's death as suicide, like most who knew her. Like Johnson, Rivera is now honoured worldwide, and her legacy is now secure. A bust of Sylvia was planned to accompany that of Marsha near the Stonewall Inn in 2021.

Thomasine *aka* Thomas Hall
(b. circa 1603)

They were born in England as Thomasine and dressed as a girl. When they were 24 years old, they cut their hair, dressed as a man and joined the army for a year as Thomas with their brother. After that, they lived as Thomasine again for a few years, before deciding to travel to America in 1627 as an indentured servant and as Thomas.

In Virginia, they started working as a man but then started to dress as a woman again. After rumours that they had sex with a maid called Bess, they were inspected by married women, who stated that they were male. However, the women made a statement that they had, 'a piece of flesh growing at the belly as big as the top of [a] little finger' and 'a piece of a hole'. Those statements indicate that they were most likely intersex, and this information was acted upon, with them being required to wear women's clothes.

The women did a second inspection and a third with one of the colony's masters, and all insisted that they were male. And they were stopped out on the road and forcibly stripped and examined by a Captain Basse and Roger Rodes, who agreed they were male.

They were brought before the general court in Richmond, Virginia, charged with masquerading as a woman and sexual misconduct (with Bess). An interesting statement they made was, 'I go in woman's apparel to get a bit for my cat' (this was women's slang for sexual intercourse – like using the modern slang 'pussy'). During their trial in 1629, they detailed their story to Governor John Pott, who declared them to be a man and a woman and, rather than allowing them to choose, made them wear men's clothes, but with a women's cap and apron. This would have made them a punishing spectacle, but there are no further records.

One Thomas Hall did die in Virginia in 1633, but another is recorded as living there into the 1640s.

Venus Barbata *or* Bearded Venus
(circa 500 BCE)

The gods and goddesses of ancient Greece, Cyprus and Rome and their worshippers were involved in transvestism as part of their rituals and worship. The male followers of Venus Barbata dressed in female clothing and may have accepted castration, and there are tales of priests committing ecstatic self-castration. In the Roman mythology, Venus was given male attributes, such as the beard, and abilities that were later given to Mars. She was often represented as having a double-sexed nature. Unusually, the name 'Venus' does have a masculine ending (with a feminine ending, it would be 'Vena').

The Spartans portrayed Venus in battle armour (as Venus Armata) and they also worshipped the form of Venus Calva (Bald Venus). Aphroditus, which is also a male name, originated in Cyprus and arrived in Athens around 400 BCE. In this guise, Aphroditus had female dress and a phallus. A surviving 4th century BCE mould for a figurine shows a dress being lifted to show male genitals. There were associated gender-swapping rituals when men and women would exchange their clothes and their behaviour. The male priests of Aphrodite Urania and Cybele also castrated themselves. Aphroditus was associated with the moon and with the power to influence the creation of vegetable and animal fertility and creation. This gender fluidity and bisexuality existed in antiquity but was prohibited and an anathema in the Christian world, a situation which has persisted for far too long.

Venus had many guises, such as the later Roman Venus Castina, who was associated with men who had feminine souls and male bodies, now defined as cross-gender. From the late 19th century, Venus Castina was associated with homosexuals and colloquially known as 'Venus of the sodomites'. Even in the antique version of astrology, there were different characteristics for the seventh and eighth houses that were influenced by Venus/Libra. These contained the male/female aspects and the powerful adult warrior woman/youthful maiden. Maybe it's time to adopt Venus as our symbol, especially in one of their many intersex identities.

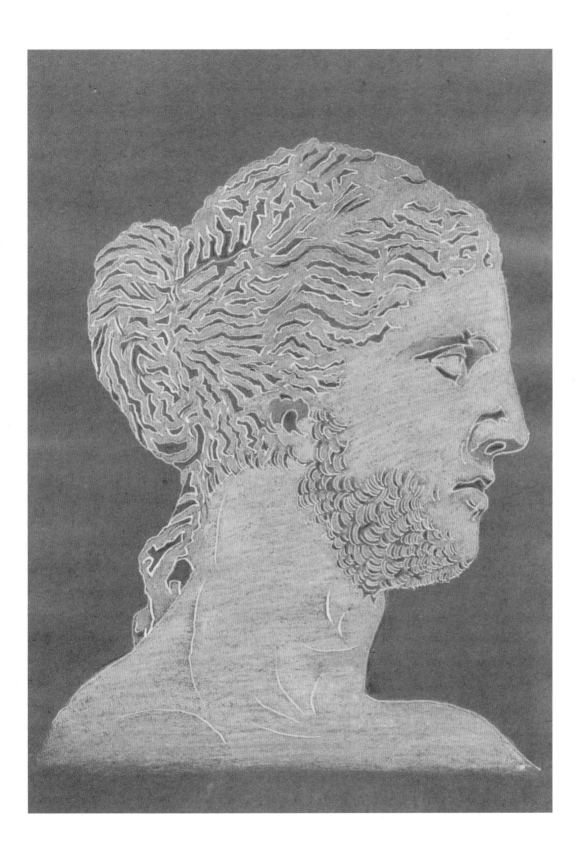

We'wha
(1849–1896)

We'wha was a third gender or lhamana Native American, born in the Zuni tribe in present-day New Mexico. The 1990s terminology for We'wha is that they were a Two-Spirit. Many tribes still have their own names for their bi-gendered individuals. The Yurok in present-day California define them as Wergerm. We'wha had a spiritual role in the tribe and was fully accepted as lhamana from a young age. They would have been taught male and female tasks and they were an especially accomplished weaver and potter whose work is displayed in museums. The Zuni were friendly to the settlers and helped them defeat the shared enemies, the Apaches and Navajos.

We'wha worked in the soldiers' fort doing domestic work, which is where an early female anthropologist called Matilda C. Stevenson found them in 1879. They were befriended by Matilda, who wrote a lot about them. She would have called We'wha a Berdache, a term less accepted by those who are third gender. She did report how respected and intelligent they were and invited We'wha to Washington in 1886. They went to President Cleveland after his recent marriage and presented him with gifts they had made and talked with him (in English). After a few months they returned home, but were arrested with five others who rebelled against the soldiers' rule and were even charged with witchcraft. At 47, We'wha died of a heart attack whilst at their Sha'lako festival.

Books about the Zuni and We'wha were written by Matilda and a contemporary, Frank Hamilton Cushing. Will Roscoe's more recent work on the Zuni and his work *Changing Ones: Third and Fourth Genders in Native North America* are all available. The latter includes many stories of warrior women and the other-gendered, such as Biawacheeitchish. Male and female Two-Spirits were called a third gender and some tribes called just female Two-Spirits a fourth gender. There is evidence that most tribes had roles for them and that the custom originated in Asia thousands of years ago, before they migrated to the Americas.

A Global History of Gender Diverse Cultures

There is no date for the first appearance of 'other gendered' indigenous people. They have always been recorded and therefore must have always existed, so why is their status and ours still in question and endangered? This book attempts to record and rescue some of our history. It is out of these traditional roles that the others I have written about in this book (and more) have descended. They suffered under colonial administrations and religious missionaries, who inflicted their own prejudices on other cultures. Unfortunately, there are current examples of some still trying to reimpose discriminatory laws (as I write this, it is happening in Ghana, which previously welcomed me). What follows should give you a flavour of the diversity of traditions that have been recorded around the world.

Currently, in Northern Australia about 80 of the 2500 of the Tiwi Aboriginal people on Bathurst and Melville Islands are transgender (also called Yimpininni, or sistergirls).

Samoa's trans men are called fa'afatama and the fa'afafine are the trans women (Steva Auina is a modern fa'afafine). They are the third and fourth genders. They host ceremonies, care for the elders and teach other Samoans about their culture. Other Polynesian countries also have their third gender populations, like the māhū of Tahiti and Hawaii (such as Kumu Hina) and the fakaleitī of Tonga (like Joey Joleen Mataele). They all maintain cultural traditions and form support groups for each other.

The gender fluid machi continue to be the shamans of the Mapuche people of southern Chile. They are also healers, artists and activists, despite being labelled as deviants by the state.

The muxes are the third gender community among the Zapotec people of Oaxaca, Mexico. They have upheld the cultural traditions and language since before colonization. The Muxe Estrella Vazquez featured on the cover of *Vogue México* in December 2019. Since the 1970s, modern South American transgender women have adopted the term travesti to define themselves.

The waria transgender women of Muslim Indonesia are an ancient community of mixed gender people, some of whom now fully transition.

The Māori of New Zealand use the term takatāpui for their LGBTQI+

people and this expresses both gender and sexual identities. The term akava'ine is now used by Cook Island Māoris to mean a transgender person and the Te Tiare Association is the island's LGBTQI+ support group.

There are many Two-Spirit traditions in America (see also Biawacheeitchish in the book). Nádleehi (one who changes) are Navajo/Diné men or intersex people who have a feminine nature. The Diné four genders include masculine women and feminine men. The artist Hosteen Klah and the subject of the documentary, *Two-Spirits*, Fred Martinez, were nádleehi.

Lhamana are also part of the Two-Spirit tradition of the Pueblo tribe and are feminine men in their Zuni culture. We'wha (earlier in this book) was a famous lhamana.

Winyanktehca is a Lakota word used by the Sioux tribe of North America. It means 'wants to be like a woman'. Shortened to winkte, it now means anyone on the LGBTQI+ spectrum.

Sipiniq are the Inuit equivalent of third gender. They include those who are intersex, but they are also believed to host the spirits of specific ancestors and to take on their gender and skills. In the late 1970s, the French anthropologist Bernard Saladin D'Anglure studied the Inuit in the Canadian Arctic and described their form of gender transition as 'perinatal transsexuality'. He also noted their increased rate of female pseudo-hermaphroditism.

Burrnesha (sworn virgins) are found in northern Albania and other Balkan countries. They are women who wear men's clothes and have taken a vow of chastity in front of elders. These societies were extremely paternalistic and traditional in outlook and limited the lives of women. In contrast, the sworn virgins live completely as men and become the heads of households and inherit. Some of the indigenous people of the Americas had a similar practice.

Koekchuch were men who behaved as women and even mistresses among the Itelmen people of Siberia. The society of the Koryaks of eastern Russia also used to keep koekchuch.

The köçek of Turkey were male dancers and musicians who dressed as females from the 17th century, in the time of the Ottoman Empire, up to the 19th century. They were recruited as very young boys from other subject countries, originally to perform in the palaces and later in taverns.

The khawal, similarly, were male dancers who dressed and performed as women in Egypt around the same time as the köçek. They both replaced women, who could not dance in public.

In Oman and parts of Arabia, khanith is a term used for trans women and any feminine men.

Tumtum is a Hebrew word that means 'hidden' and was used to define people who had confusing genitalia. It was used in Jewish Rabbinic literature for genitals that needed some surgery in order to have sex. Modern equivalents could be intersex and transgender. Classic Judaism defined multiple genders, including tumtum. They also include male, female, saris (eunuch, or born male and more female), androgynos (both male and female) and aylonit (female at birth and later becoming more male). Two of the early Jewish figures, according to some experts, were transitioned. One was Abraham's son Isaac, who was to be female, but was changed to be born male in order to fulfil the prophecies. The other was Dinah, Jacob's daughter, divinely changed into a female.

The Hebrew Genesis Rabbah, written sometime in the 3rd and 5th centuries, and the 11th century commentator, Shlomo Yitzhaki (also called Rashi) both share the same comments on the biblical creation myth. They and others state that Adam was formed as an androgynos and only when Eve was made from a rib did they become male and female. Some modern scholars, including Rabbi Elliot Kukla, also say that the line 'God created Adam in His image, in the image of God He created him; male and female God created them' in Genesis means that the first human was androgynous.

The Anatolian mother goddess, Cybele, possibly originated as early as 600 BCE and was adopted by the Greeks in 300 BCE and later by the Romans. Her mendicant priests (the galli) castrated themselves and wore make-up and jewellery whilst dressing and behaving as women. The goddess became established and grew in importance and influence. In 2002, excavations of a Roman fort in North Yorkshire revealed the buried remains of a 400 CE galla in women's clothes and jewellery. Nearby Hadrian's Wall also has an altar to Cybele.

In Eurasia, the nomadic Scythian people worshipped Aphrodite, who was Venus for the Romans. Both Venus Castina and the earlier Venus Barbata had, as disciples, men who had a feminine nature. Shamans, called enarees (effeminate or androgynous disciples) made use of entheogens (hallucinogens) to achieve religious ecstasy.

Chibados were men who lived as women amongst the Ndongo of Angola. They were shamans and performed services and burials. They were respected and could marry the Ndongo men. The Portuguese introduced homophobia into Angola when they colonized it. The Bugis ethnic group of Indonesians believed that everything had a distinct spiritual essence, which is termed animism. Most now are Muslim, but their earlier cultural beliefs continue to be respected. These include the concept of five and not two genders, which is also shared by the hijras of

India (like Laxmi Narayan Tripathi), Bangladesh and Pakistan (like Kami Sid), the Kathoey and phuying of Thailand (like Treechada Petcharat) and the mak nyah in Malaysia. Their five genders are calalai (trans men), calabai (trans women), bissu (intersex/androgynous), oroané (cisgender men) and makkunrai (cisgender women). The bissu may be of a spiritually, rather than physically, mixed gender. They still perform important cultural duties and religious ceremonies, though they are subject to harassment by Islamists.

The Filipinos use the terms baklâ, bayot and agî in different regional languages, and they all refer to men who present as female. They now face discrimination from some (Jennifer Laude was killed by an American soldier in 2014). Women presenting as male are named as binalaki and lakin-on). In Buddhist Myanmar, the apwint are transgender women. However, they face severe penalties for merely existing because of Section 377 of the British colonial penal code, which was kept after Burmese independence (as has happened in other former colonies). Though it was intended to prohibit certain sexual acts, it is used to persecute any apwint at any time.

Femminielli continue to exist in the poor Quartieri Spagnoli (Spanish Quarter) of Naples, where they have always been accepted. They present as female and are classed as third gender, rather than transgender. There is a comic painting, 'Il Femminiello', painted by Giuseppe Bonito in the mid-18th century. Ketty Gabriele, a local mafia boss in charge of prostitution and drugs, was arrested in 2009. She was a femminielli, but was also described as transgender and a cross-dresser, as well as being dead-named.

I hope that this brief list of some of the sex and gender presentations that have occurred in different times and places provides some background and context to the individual stories that are included.

Trans Awareness Dates

Global Pride Day is on 27th June.
(Brenda Howard organized a Stonewall anniversary rally in July 1969, after the riots, and the next year planned Gay Pride Week and the Christopher Street Liberation Day Parade.)

Transgender Day of Remembrance is on 20th November.
(It was founded in 1999 by Gwendolyn Ann Smith to honour Rita Hester, an African American transgender woman, who was murdered in Allston, Massachusetts.)

Transgender Day of Visibility is on 31st March.
(It is an international event to celebrate transgender people and to raise awareness of the discrimination of them.)

Intersex Awareness Day is on 26th October.
(The first public demonstration in the USA by intersex people was held on this day in 1996 at the annual conference of the American Academy of Paediatrics, with Morgan Holmes and Max Black, who were refused permission to speak.)

Intersex Day of Solidarity is on 8th November.
(This is Herculine Barbin's birthday and is also **International Day of Remembrance**. The intersex flag was added to the combined Pride flag in 2021.)

Non-Binary Celebration and Awareness Week is 12th to 18th July.
(This includes **International Non-Binary People's Day** on 14 July and is between International Men's Day, 19th November, and International Women's Day, 8th March.)

Index

Transitions

Our Stories of Being Trans
Various Authors

Forewords by Meg-John Barker,
Juno Roche and Sabah Choudrey

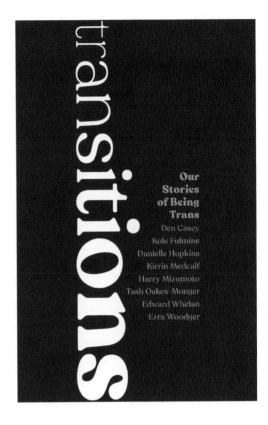

A visionary, moving and one-of-a-kind anthology of writing on what it means to be trans today and every day.

From the daily bite of anxiety as you go to leave the house, to the freedom found swimming in the wild, through to moments of queer rage and joy and the peculiar timeslip of reliving your adolescence, the stories in this collection reveal the untold lived realities of trans people to help inform, inspire and unite. Spanning a range of topics such as gender dysphoria, transphobia, chest binding, gender reassignment surgery, coming out in later life, migration, and love and relationships, these unique first-person accounts celebrate the beauty and diversity of being trans and will empower others on their journey. Showcasing eight exciting new trans writers, this extraordinary collection is a powerful and heartfelt love letter to the trans community.

Includes contributions from the winners of the inaugural JKP Writing Prize:

Den Casey
Kole Fulmine
Danielle Hopkins
Kirrin Medcalf
Harry Mizumoto
Tash Oakes-Monger
Edward Whelan
Ezra Woodger

£12.99 | $18.95 | PB | 112PP
ISBN 978 1 78775 851 3 | EISBN 978 1 78775 852 0

The A–Z of Gender and Sexuality

From Ace to Ze
Morgan Lev Edward Holleb

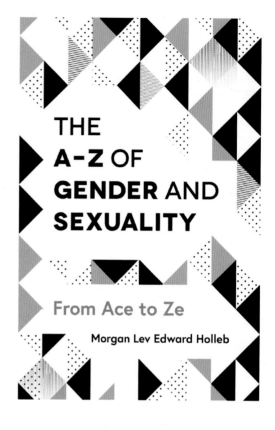

There can be confusion around the appropriate terminology for trans and queer identities, even within the trans community itself. As language is constantly evolving, it can be difficult to know what to say. As a thorough A–Z glossary of trans and queer words from "A" to "zucchini," this dictionary guide will help to dispel anxiety around using the "wrong" words, while explaining the weight of using certain labels and providing individuals with a vocabulary for personal identification. Written in a traditional A–Z glossary style, this guide will serve as a quick reference for looking up individual words, as well as an in-depth look at queer history and culture.

Morgan Lev Edward Holleb is a queer anarchist and an advocate for LGBT+ healthcare in Scotland. He runs a support group called Not Your Fault for men and nonbinary people who have experienced sexual violence. He plays the cello and likes plants.

£16.99 | $22.95 | PB | 344PP

ISBN 978 1 78592 342 5 | EISBN 978 1 78450 663 6